The RESENTMENT YEARS

When Desire Becomes Duty

MINA V. ADLER

Author of Die Alone, Then

MINERVA DOY
PUBLISHING

Paperback ISBN: 978-1-7646319-0-7

Hardcover ISBN: 978-1-7646319-1-4

Ebook ISBN: 978-1-7646319-2-1

For Kirstie

O persistently lingering sproggle, whose unwavering exchanges have resulted in the inadvertent transfer of semi-useful knowledge, I note that your continued existence within my communicative radius is not wholly without merit.

THE RESENTMENT YEARS

When Desire Becomes Duty

Mina V. Adler

MINERVA DOY
PUBLISHING

Minerva Doy Publishing

You do not lose yourself all at once.

Contents

Introduction   1

PART I: Before Desire Becomes Duty   5

1. The Partnership Belief   7

2. Being Chosen as the Prize   13

3. Read This Before You Move In   21

4. When Connection Becomes Exchange   27

5. Performing for Retention   35

PART II: The Shift   43

6. The Woman Who Loved Well   47

7. The Good Wife Script   59

8. Emotional Infrastructure   71

9. The Competence Trap   81

10. Death by Accommodation   91

11. Sex as Insurance   101

12. And So She Tries   111

13. The Slow Slide   115

PART III: When It No Longer Feels Like Love   127

14. The Silent Scorecard   131

15. Sex as Obligation   139

16. The Panic of Missing Out   151

17. When Desire Became Duty   159

18. The Loss of Respect   169

19. The Loneliness Inside Marriage   177

PART IV: The Breaking Point   183

20. The Fight Wasn't About the Dishes   187

21. The In-Between   195

22. Divorce as Detox?   203

23. The Rage Stage   211

PART V: After the Pattern   217

24. No Longer Trying to Be Chosen   223

25. Refusing to Manage What Is Not Hers   229

26. Desire Is Not Negotiable   235

27. Paying Attention to the Shift   245

28. The Liberation of Doing Less, and Watching What Happens   249

29. Not Staying to See If It Gets Better   255

30. Being Willing to Lose the Relationship   261

31. Recognizing the Pattern, Not the Person   267

32. Self-Trust After Resentment   273

33. No Longer Living in Disappearance   279

Afterword   285

About the Author   289

Introduction

You didn't become resentful overnight.

You became resentful slowly. Politely. Responsibly. With the best of intentions.

In *The Resentment Years: When Desire Becomes Duty*, we will examine the quiet transformation many women experience inside long relationships and marriages.

It did not begin as a problem.

It began as love. As generosity. As attentiveness. A willingness to meet someone halfway, to keep things steady, to build something that lasts.

But over time, something shifted.

What once felt natural begins to feel managed. What once felt mutual becomes uneven.

Then, one day, something that once felt like love...feels like work.

And the relationship—even the one that looks perfectly stable from the outside—gradually takes on weight: obligation, maintenance, and a silent exhaustion.

Eventually, quieter questions emerge.

Why do capable, intelligent women find themselves carrying the emotional weight of entire relationships?

What happens when devotion becomes labor—and when that labor is invisible?

This book examines that shift—not as a failure of love, but as the result of a structure; one that rewards women for adapting, stabilizing, and carrying what is not entirely theirs.

We explore the moment when love begins to feel like labor, and intimacy—sex—begins to feel like obligation.

We question the invisible expectations that shape modern relationships, especially the subtle pressure many women feel to maintain sexual availability in order to preserve connection and prevent distance.

Drawing on cultural insight, psychological clarity, and unflinching honesty, we expose the quiet contract many women inherit: the belief that if they are loving enough, patient enough, and sexually generous enough, the relationship will remain secure.

This is not a book about blaming men or shaming women.

It is about seeing clearly, and understanding the patterns that quietly drain love of its vitality—so they can be replaced with something more powerful: clarity, self-respect, and emotional sovereignty.

Once the pattern is visible, something else becomes possible.

Not perfection. Not control.

But the ability to stop building relationships that require you to disappear inside them.

Part warning for younger women and part recognition for those who have already lived it, *The Resentment Years* speaks directly to the generation of women now asking a difficult question:

When did desire become duty?

For any woman who has ever wondered how love turned into work, this book offers recognition, relief, and a way forward.

Because the resentment years do not have to be the for the rest of your life.

PART 1: Before Desire Becomes Duty

There is a version of love that exists before anything has gone wrong.

It is hopeful, generous, and quietly certain that effort will be returned in kind.

This is where most women begin.

Where being chosen feels like safety, where intimacy feels natural, and where the small adjustments that sustain connection still feel like love.

And it is here, in these early stages, that something almost invisible begins.

A shift so gradual it is rarely named.

Not conflict. Not imbalance.

Adaptation.

A growing awareness of how to keep things smooth. A subtle instinct to be easy, to be understanding, to be someone who can be loved without friction.

Nothing about this seems dangerous. If anything, it feels right.

But over time, these small adjustments begin to form a pattern.

This is where it starts.

Not with resentment—but with love that slowly learns to perform itself.

In these opening chapters, we examine the early years of modern relationships:

The pull of being chosen.

The subtle pressure to be accommodating.

And the slow introduction of intimacy as something to be maintained rather than felt.

Before the resentment, there was hope.

Before the exhaustion, there was effort.

And before love began to feel like work, there was a quiet set of beliefs most women never question—until it is too late.

Chapter 1

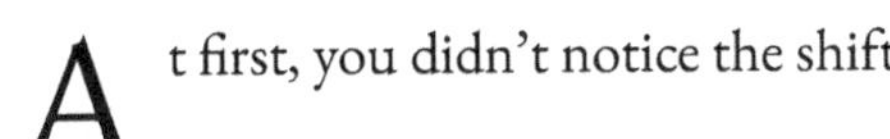

At first, you didn't notice the shift.

You loved him. You were generous with your time, your attention, and your body.

Intimacy felt natural—part of the connection you were building together.

But slowly, something changed.

Sex became reassurance.

Affection became maintenance.

And the relationship you once entered with desire began to feel like something you had to manage.

This book will help you understand how it happens—and how to ensure it doesn't define the rest of your life.

This is not anti-men, anti-marriage, anti-sex.

It is *anti-self-abandonment.*

You are exposing the myth that a woman must *earn* stability by being useful.

The Belief

There is a particular kind of woman this book is for, and her age is not a factor.

She did not enter love naïvely. She entered it sincerely.

She believed in partnership. She believed in building something with someone. She believed that if two adults treated each other well, communicated honestly, and stayed loyal to the project of the relationship, things would work.

She was not careless with people's feelings. She was not manipulative. She did not play games with anyone.

In fact, she tried very hard not to.

She prided herself on being reasonable. Reasonable during disagreements. Reasonable when things were uneven for a while. Reasonable when she carried a little more than her share.

After all, relationships required compromise.

That is what she had always been told.

And so she compromised. Not dramatically. Not in a way that would alarm anyone from the outside.

The adjustments were small. A cancelled plan. A softened reaction. A moment of silence instead of saying what she really felt.

Nothing remarkable. Nothing alarming.

Just the slow smoothing of the relationship's rough edges.

This is how the resentment years begin.

Not with a betrayal. Not with cruelty.

But with accommodation.

Beneath the Belief

Underneath all of this was a simple idea.

If she was loving enough, the relationship would be secure.

Be supportive. Be affectionate. Be easy to be around.

And in return, she would be valued.

The message is rarely stated outright, but it is reinforced constantly.

Women learn early that being desirable is an advantage, but being *difficult* is a liability.

They learn that men like women who are fun, spontaneous, uncomplicated. Women who don't complain too much. Women who are enthusiastic about intimacy. Women who don't make everything heavy.

And so they try to become someone who is easy to love.

When Effort Becomes Structure

At first, this works. The relationship feels stable, connected, functional.

But over time, something subtle happens.

The effort she offers becomes part of the structure.

She notices more. Adjusts more. Carries slightly more.

And because she does it well, it becomes invisible.

The Beginning of the Pattern

Nothing has gone wrong. There is no betrayal. No rupture.

But the balance has shifted.

She is no longer just participating in the relationship.

She is maintaining it.

And this does not yet feel like a problem.

It still feels like love.

The First Cost

What she does not see, at least not immediately, is that this pattern has a direction.

It requires her to continue adjusting, smoothing, holding things steady.

And over time, that effort accumulates.

Not as anger—but as fatigue.

Transition

And because this pattern begins so quietly, it is easy to miss where it first takes hold.

Not in conflict.

But in the early experience of love itself.

Chapter 2

Being Chosen As The Prize

(And Why You Walked Into It Willingly)

Before she became resentful, she was chosen.

And that mattered more than she realized at the time.

Not because she was insecure. Not because she lacked self-worth.

But because being chosen had always carried meaning.

It meant she was wanted. Desired.

It meant, perhaps most importantly, that she was not alone.

For many women, this is where the story truly begins.

Not with love—but with selection.

The Early Conditioning

From a young age, girls learn, quietly and indirectly, that being chosen is a form of success.

They may be encouraged to pursue independence and ambition.

But alongside those messages runs another current: Be likeable. Be attractive. Be calm.

Be the kind of girl someone would pick.

This is not always taught explicitly. It does not need to be.

It is reinforced in smaller ways.

The agreeable girl is praised. The low-drama girl is preferred. The girl who does not make things difficult is described as a catch.

By adolescence, most girls understand: Attention can be earned—and, more importantly, lost.

The Beginning of the Validation Economy

Approval is not distributed evenly. It is responsive.

You learn what gets rewarded: Smiling more than you feel. Laughing when something isn't funny. Not pushing too hard when something bothers you.

Being "cool." Being relaxed. Being the woman who doesn't require too much explanation.

She does not think of herself as performing. She thinks of herself as being likeable.

These adjustments feel small. Harmless, even.

But over time, they shape behavior. Because what is rewarded is repeated.

When She Is Chosen

By the time she begins dating, she is already fluent in this.

She is warm, attentive, flexible, understanding.

And when a man chooses her—really chooses her, with enthusiasm and focus—it feels like confirmation.

That she is enough. That she is desirable. That she has, in some quiet way, succeeded.

Why Intensity Feels Like Safety

Early intensity amplifies this feeling.

The long messages. The constant attention. The sense that he cannot get enough of her.

It feels like certainty. Like safety. Like something settled.

It feels like the opposite of all the ambiguity she has been warned about.

But intensity is not stability. It only looks like it.

And is therefore easier to mistake for something deeper.

The Quiet Pressure

There is another force at work here, one that is rarely named directly: Competition.

Even women who do not think of themselves as competitive feel its presence.

The awareness—sometimes faint, sometimes sharp—that there are other women. Other options. Other possibilities.

This creates a subtle pressure to maintain position. To remain interesting. To remain desirable. To remain easy to choose again.

Because being chosen once never feels permanent—it feels conditional.

This awareness does not need to be dramatic to be effective. It only needs to exist.

The Invisible Shift

This is where "being chill" becomes valuable.

The woman who does not overreact. The woman who does not question too much. The woman who does not make demands too early.

She is seen as safe. Not emotionally unsafe. Relationally low-risk.

She will not disrupt the connection. She will not complicate things. She will not force decisions before he is ready.

And so she is rewarded. With continued attention. With proximity. With the sense that she is doing the relationship correctly.

But something important is happening beneath the surface.

She is learning that her position is maintained not by who she is—but by how she behaves.

This distinction is easy to miss.

Because the outcomes feel the same.

He stays.
He calls.
He chooses her again.

But the mechanism is different.

And over time, that difference matters.

The Myth of Irreplaceability

It begins here.

She believes—often unconsciously—that if she is good enough, he will not want anyone else.

That if she is attractive enough, easy enough, generous enough, she will become uniquely valuable to him.

Difficult to leave.

Hard to replace.

This belief is comforting. It suggests control. It suggests that the outcome of the relationship rests, at least in part, in her hands.

But it rests on a fragile assumption: That being chosen is the same as being valued.

They are not the same.

Being Chosen vs Being Valued

Being chosen is an event. Being valued is a pattern that unfolds over time.

Being chosen can happen quickly. Being valued is gradually revealed.

Being chosen often depends on attraction, timing, and availability. Being valued depends on character, consistency, and care.

But early in relationships, these distinctions are not always visible.

Because the feeling of being chosen is powerful.

It quiets doubt. It creates momentum. It makes the relationship feel established before it has actually been tested.

And so she invests. Emotionally. Practically. Sexually.

Not because she is calculating—but because she feels secure. Because being chosen has given her that feeling.

What she does not yet see is that the security she feels is not always rooted in reality.

It is rooted in perception. In attention. In momentum. In the absence of threat.

Over time, this becomes important.

Because when the relationship inevitably shifts—as all relationships do—the foundation is tested.

And if the foundation was built on being chosen, rather than being deeply valued, something begins to feel unstable.

Attention fluctuates. Effort becomes inconsistent. Certainty softens.

Where the Pattern Takes Hold

When the relationship inevitably shifts, she adjusts.

To regain what she believes has been lost.

Because the woman who learned to be chosen will often work to stay chosen.

She softens. Gives more. Becomes more accommodating.

Not dramatically. Just enough to restore balance. Just enough to feel secure again.

But security built on being chosen is never truly stable. Because it depends on continued selection.

And continued selection always carries the possibility of deselection.

What This Chapter Is Saying

Women in their thirties and forties can often see this clearly with hindsight.

They can trace the arc. The early certainty. The gradual adjustment. The quiet increase in effort.

They can see how much of their behavior was shaped not by who they were—but by what they believed would keep the relationship intact.

And they can see, often with surprising clarity, the moment they confused attention with investment. Selection with value. Intensity with safety.

The Final Truth

If you are younger, this chapter is not a warning against being loved.

It is a warning against misunderstanding what love looks like.

Being chosen feels good. It should.

But it is not, on its own, evidence of anything lasting.

The question is not whether he chose you.

The question is how he treats you once you are no longer new.

Because that is where value is revealed.

And that is where the resentment years either begin—or are quietly avoided.

Chapter 3

READ THIS BEFORE YOU MOVE IN

M oving in together is rarely treated as a risk.

It is treated as progress.

A milestone. A sign of commitment. A natural next step.

It often arrives wrapped in optimism.

You'll spend more time together. You'll share lives. You'll feel closer, more connected, more certain.

It feels like consolidation. Like taking something good and making it stronger.

You want it to work.

The Threshold No One Names

But moving in is not just a romantic step.

It is structural.

It changes the dynamic of a relationship in ways that are not always visible at first.

You are now managing each other.

And that is where things begin to shift.

The Change from Girlfriend to Infrastructure

Before you lived together, your presence in his life was contained.

You saw each other deliberately. Time together was chosen. Effort was visible.

When you leave that structure behind, something subtle happens.

You become ambient in his life.

Because once you share a space, you are no longer a planned experience; you are part of each other's environment.

And with that shift comes an unspoken upgrade in responsibility.

Not formally. Not consciously. But functionally.

The Quiet Expansion

You begin to notice more.

The logistics. The emotional tone of the home. The small things that keep life running. The dishes. The laundry. The groceries.

You begin to anticipate needs. You smooth things over before they become issues. You think ahead.

And because you are capable, you do it well—almost too well.

So well, in fact, that it disappears from view.

Chosen Is Not Cherished

Being chosen got you here. It will not sustain you.

Because cohabitation tests something different.

Not attraction. Not chemistry. Not even compatibility in the way you once understood it.

It tests contribution. Effort. Responsibility.

And above all, regard.

The way he treats you when you are no longer new.

The way he responds when there is no performance, no anticipation, no novelty to sustain the connection.

Being chosen feels like security.

But being cherished is something else entirely.

It is slower. Quieter. Less performative.

And far more revealing.

The Critical Question

Not: "Do we love each other?"

Not: "Do we get along?"

Not even: "Are we compatible?"

The real question is: *Am I already adjusting myself to keep this relationship stable?*

Because if the answer is yes, living together will not fix it. It will deepen it.

Moving In Doesn't Create the Problem—It Reveals It
Cohabitation doesn't cause this dynamic.

It exposes it.

Because proximity removes illusion. It reveals effort, imbalance, and who carries what.

And once you are inside the same space, the patterns are revealed and amplified.

What was occasional becomes regular, what was subtle becomes structural.

Before You Cross the Threshold
If you are young, this chapter is a warning.

If you are older, it is a recognition.

Either way, it offers the same instruction:

Do not move in while you are still performing.

Do not build a shared life on unspoken adjustments.

Do not confuse being chosen with being secure.

Because what you are already compensating for will only become more visible once you are living inside it.

Once duty enters the relationship, it does not stay quiet for long.

Chapter 4

WHEN CONNECTION BECOMES EXCHANGE

I n the beginning, it does feel different.

The early years of love are full of possibility. Conversation feels easy. There is curiosity, discovery, the electricity of mutual attraction.

Intimacy feels natural, spontaneous and generous – like an extension of connection rather than a negotiation.

Nothing needs to be managed. It unfolds on its own.

If you are young, in love, and reading this book, you may find the women in these pages puzzling.

You may read about relationships where sex became mechanical, about wives who felt obligated rather than eager, about women quietly dreading intimacy with men they once adored.

You might wonder how that happens.

How does desire—so intense at the beginning—turn into something negotiated, scheduled, or endured?

How does the woman who once wanted him suddenly feel like she is fulfilling a responsibility?

How does something that was once *connection* somehow become an *exchange?*

At twenty-two, the answer seems simple: She chose badly. She stayed too long. She stopped trying.

You assume you will do it differently.

Most women have made this assumption.

They believe love will remain vibrant if the relationship is healthy, if communication is good, if both partners are emotionally intelligent adults.

They believe sexual connection will remain natural as long as they stay open-minded and affectionate.

Leaning In

They believe that if things begin to feel slightly off in a relationship, they would not withdraw.

They would lean in.

They would become more attentive. More accommodating. More understanding. More generous.

This feels like the right response.

After all, if something is slipping, it should be stabilized. If distance is emerging, it should be closed.

And one of the fastest ways to restore closeness is through intimacy.

So they offer it.

Not always consciously. Not always reluctantly.

But consistently enough that a pattern begins to form.

At that point, quietly, something changes.

Another idea begins to creep in. Not dramatically. Not all at once.

A small moment.

It rarely arrives as a rule. It arrives as a suggestion.

The suggestion that a woman must *earn* stability by being useful.

The suggestion that if you want the relationship to stay strong, you must remain generous with your body.

And so young women begin to internalize something that feels like maturity.

They absorb this idea early. Sometimes from friends. Sometimes from magazines and podcasts. Sometimes from the men they date. Sometimes simply from the ambient culture that surrounds them.

The advice often sounds modern and liberating.

Be sex-positive.
Don't be uptight.
Don't withhold intimacy when you're upset.
Men have needs.

These statements are often presented as enlightened relationship wisdom.

But beneath them sits a quieter implication: *maintaining a man's sexual satisfaction is a stabilising force in the relationship.*

If intimacy slows down, the relationship might drift.

If a partner feels rejected too often, he might become distant.

If distance grows, someone else could enter the picture.

None of this is usually stated so bluntly. It is simply understood.

There'll Be a First Time for This Scenario

You're making a sandwich. Lost in your thoughts.

He embraces you gently from behind.

You stop what you're doing but you don't turn around.

He nuzzles you.

You hesitate for a moment. You joke about how "insatiable" he is.

He murmurs, "Come on, you know you'll like it."

You keep hesitating.

Not because you don't love him. Not because you don't care.

But because you don't quite want to begin. You just want to finish the sandwich. You just want to continue being lost in your thoughts.

You turn around.

You oblige.

It feels insignificant.

But it is the first time something has been overridden.

And it occurs to you: Sex is not always about pleasure. Sometimes it is maintenance.

The First "Yes" That Isn't Fully Yours

By the time many women reach their thirties or forties, they can look back and identify that moment.

Not dramatic.

Not even memorable at the time.

Just a small hesitation.

A brief internal pause.

A moment where they were not entirely in the mood.

And then—They said yes. Not unhappily. Not resentfully.

Just... gently overriding themselves.

Because it seemed easier. Because it seemed kind. Because it seemed like the right thing to do.

What That Moment Teaches

That moment does not stand alone.

It becomes part of a quiet understanding.

That closeness sometimes requires effort.

That saying no too often creates distance.

That maintaining connection may require participation, even when desire is not fully present.

None of this is stated directly.

But it is absorbed.

A Transaction Has Begun

Sometimes a shift becomes visible in other small, telling ways.

A joke. A comment. A pattern of language.

"I'll take out the trash—I got lucky last night."

It is said lightly.

But something in it lands heavily.

Because what was once a connection is now being framed as an *exchange:* I'll do this for you if you do something in return.

And once intimacy becomes transactional, something fundamental has already changed.

Chapter 5

PERFORMING FOR RETENTION

Over time, these moments of expectation and feelings of exchange repeat.

Not constantly. Just occasionally. And because they are occasional, they do not feel like a problem.

This is how patterns form.

But, gradually, something shifts.

The Subtlety of the Shift
At first the shift is subtle.

She still enjoys intimacy much of the time. She still feels close to him. She still believes the relationship is strong.

But gradually the balance tilts.

The number of times she initiates because she wants to begins to decline.

The number of times she participates because it seems easier than refusing begins to rise.

She does not call this obligation. She calls it love.

And because she calls it love, she rarely questions it.

The Role Expands

She is still a lover—but she becomes something else as well.

A stabilizer.

Someone who keeps closeness intact, even when it does not arise naturally.

And again, this does not feel wrong. It feels like being a good partner.

And underneath that instinct to maintain connection is something deeper.

Not just care.

But the desire to remain chosen.

When Intimacy Becomes Performance

Women in their thirties and forties know where this road leads.

They remember when intimacy began to feel strangely performative.

Not always unpleasant. But not entirely real.

They know the quiet resentment that appears when *affection feels expected,* rather than chosen.

They know the strange contradiction of lying beside someone you care about while wishing, occasionally, that the evening would simply end.

Maintaining the Relationship

It may have been a conversation with friends about "keeping the spark alive."

It may have been advice from a relationship column about meeting your partner halfway.

Or it may have been something simpler: the quiet realisation that saying no too often seemed to create tension.

And so they said yes.

Not dramatically. Not even unhappily.

Just occasionally when they were tired.

Occasionally when they would have preferred to be doing something else.

Occasionally because they sensed his mood shifting and wanted to smooth the evening.

Each moment felt insignificant.

But this is how patterns take shape. And over time, something subtle happened.

Sex stopped being purely about desire.

It became reassurance.

Reassuring him.

Reassuring the relationship.

Reassuring themselves that everything was still fine.

At twenty-five, this arrangement barely registers.

At thirty-five, many women begin to feel its weight.

At forty-five, some can see it with painful clarity.

She was no longer simply a lover. She had become a caretaker of emotional stability.

The groundwork for resentment is already being laid. And sex had become one of the tools.

Why the Good Ones Are Most at Risk

This does not happen in every relationship. But it happens often enough that many women recognize the story immediately.

And it happens most frequently to women who tried hardest to be good partners:

Women who were emotionally intelligent.

Women who were generous.

Women who believed in fairness, effort, and reciprocity.

Women who thought devotion created safety.

The Language of Love Masks the Reality of Fear

If you are a younger woman reading this, it is important to say something clearly.

Sexual generosity is not the problem. Love often includes generosity. It includes compromise. It includes moments where we show up for a partner even when we are tired or distracted.

The problem is not kindness.

The problem is *fear*.

When intimacy begins to serve as insurance against abandonment, it stops being free.

When a woman feels responsible for maintaining a man's desire, something essential changes inside her.

Desire does not survive long under obligation.

Your Emotional Responsibility

This book is not an argument against sex. It is not an argument against men. And it is certainly not an argument against love.

It is an examination of something far quieter and more complicated: the moment when love begins to turn into labor.

The moment when emotional responsibility becomes uneven.

The moment when desire—once spontaneous—becomes a task attached to the role of partner or wife.

Those are the beginnings of the resentment years.

For some women, those years last only briefly.

For others, they stretch across decades.

By the time many women recognize them, the resentment has already done its quiet work.

Respect has thinned.

Attraction has cooled.

Exhaustion has settled into the bones of the relationship.

And the woman who once loved generously finds herself wondering: When did love become *work?*

When Love Starts Feeling Like a Job

If you are young, this book is a warning.

If you are older, it is an explanation.

Either way, it begins with the same insight:

Desire cannot survive where duty quietly takes its place.

The Final Truth

Desire does not survive maintenance.

It does not thrive under obligation.

And it cannot grow in a space where it is quietly expected.

Before you move in, you must know this: The trap is not partnership.

The trap is *performing for retention*.

And the truth is that the performance will not save you.

PART II: THE SHIFT

When Love Becomes Labor

It does not happen all at once.

There is no clear dividing line between the relationship you entered and the one you find yourself maintaining.

No single moment where love ends and something heavier takes its place.

Instead, there is a shift. Subtle at first. Reasonable, even.

You give a little more because it seems necessary.
You adjust because it feels mature.
You take on more because you are capable.

And because you are capable, you do not notice how much you have taken on.

This is the stage where good women become tired women.

Not because they loved the wrong person.

But because they slowly became responsible for things that were never meant to be carried alone.

The emotional tone of the relationship.
The repair after conflict.
The continuity of intimacy.
The quiet work of keeping everything running smoothly.

None of these roles are formally assigned.

They are absorbed.

At first, it feels like care.

Then it feels like effort.

Then, eventually, it feels like work.

This section traces that transformation.

How a woman who loved well becomes the emotional infrastructure of a relationship.

How competence becomes a trap.

How small accommodations accumulate into something larger than they appear.

And how intimacy—once spontaneous—begins to function as reassurance, repair, and, eventually, obligation.

Nothing here is dramatic.

That is precisely the problem.

Because what happens slowly is rarely questioned. And what is rarely questioned is often repeated.

By the time the shift is visible, it is already established.

By the time it has a name, it has already taken something with it.

Energy. Ease. *Desire.*

This is where love begins to change form.

Not disappear. But harden.

Into something structured, maintained, and quietly unequal.

Part I was about how the pattern begins.

Part II is about how it takes hold.

And why so many women do not recognize it — until they are already carrying it.

Chapter 6

The Woman Who Loved Well

She was not foolish.

It is important to begin there, because when a relationship ends in exhaustion—when a woman looks back and sees how much she carried, how much she adjusted, how much she gave—there is a temptation to rewrite her as naïve.

Too trusting. Too accommodating. Too willing to believe in something that was never stable.

But that is not who she was.

She was thoughtful. Capable. Someone who took love seriously.

She Did Not Enter Lightly

She did not stumble into the relationship without awareness. She paid attention. She listened, asked questions, noticed how he behaved—not just with her, but with the world around him.

She was not careless with her life.

If anything, she was deliberate.

She chose someone she believed she could build with, someone she respected, someone who felt, at least at the beginning, safe.

And once she chose, she committed. Not out of obligation, but out of intention.

She was not playing a game. She was trying to create something real.

The Belief Beneath Her Effort

Underneath her approach to love was a belief so familiar it rarely felt like a belief at all:

If I am good, love will stay.

Not perfect. Not flawless. Just good.

Kind, supportive, loyal, understanding.

She believed relationships were sustained through effort and goodwill—that if two people cared enough, they would make it work.

This did not feel naïve. It felt responsible.

Like the adult alternative to impulsiveness or indifference.

It gave her direction. It suggested that the outcome of the relationship was not random, but shaped by how she showed up.

Where That Belief Comes From

Most women do not arrive at this idea through conscious reflection.

They absorb it.

They see it in families where women hold things together—smoothing over tension, adapting when necessary, giving more when the relationship becomes strained.

They see it in stories where love is preserved through patience, endurance, quiet persistence.

The women who do this are not described as depleted.

They are described as strong.

And so strength becomes associated with endurance—with absorbing discomfort without destabilizing the relationship, with keeping things intact.

Strength, Turned Inward

Her strength is real.

It allows her to remain calm under pressure, to think clearly during conflict, to support someone she loves even when things are not perfect.

These are not weaknesses. They are what make relationships possible.

But in the wrong dynamic, strength does not remain shared.

It concentrates.

Instead of being balanced, it is leaned on.

Instead of being mutual, it becomes directional.

And over time, it carries more than it should.

Why Capable Women Do More

There is a reason this pattern appears most often in capable women.

Because they *can*.

They notice what needs to be done—and they do it.

They see gaps and fill them. They sense tension and respond before it escalates. They do not wait for problems to become obvious. They resolve them early, quietly, efficiently.

And because they do it well, the system adjusts around them.

The Formation of Roles

In any relationship, roles emerge through repetition.

If one person consistently initiates difficult conversations, she becomes the one who handles communication.

If one person restores connection after conflict, she becomes responsible for repair.

If one person maintains emotional closeness, she becomes the keeper of intimacy.

These roles are rarely discussed.

But once established, they tend to persist.

Not because they're fair—but because they work.

The Expansion She Did Not See

She did not notice when her role expanded, because each step made sense.

Of course she would bring it up—she communicates well.
Of course she would smooth things over—she dislikes tension.
Of course she would check in—she cares.

Each action was reasonable on its own. Together, they formed a pattern.

A pattern in which she became responsible not just for herself, but for the relationship itself.

From Partner to Regulator

Over time, her role shifted.

She was no longer simply participating in the relationship. She was regulating it.

She monitored its health, noticed when something was off, adjusted to restore balance, anticipated problems before they emerged.

Because she was good at this, the relationship appeared stable.

From the outside, it worked.

The Cost of Making It Work

But this kind of stability is not neutral. It is maintained—and she is the one maintaining it.

She initiates the conversations, repairs disconnection, sustains intimacy, manages the emotional undercurrents.

None of this is explicitly required, but all of it becomes expected.

And once it is expected, it becomes invisible.

Why She Didn't Stop

It is easy, from the outside, to ask why she did not step back. Why she did not demand more. Why she did not see what was happening.

But from her perspective, nothing had clearly broken.

There was no defining moment where the relationship failed. Just a gradual increase in effort

And effort, in relationships, is normal.

Expected, even.

So she did not see over-functioning.

She saw commitment.

The Myth That Sustains It

At the center of this pattern is a powerful idea: If I do this well enough, it will work.

Not if we both show up equally, not if he meets me here. But if *I* handle this properly—if *I* communicate clearly enough, give enough—things will stabilize.

This belief suggests that the relationship's outcome is not entirely outside her influence.

That her effort matters.

Devotion and Control

This can look like devotion. But it also functions as control.

Not control over him—but over the trajectory of the relationship.

If she is the one holding things together, then she is the one preventing them from falling apart.

This is reassuring. But it is also a burden.

Because it places the weight of the relationship, quietly and persistently, on her.

When Effort Becomes Identity

Over time, her role becomes part of who she is.

She is the understanding one. The patient one. The emotionally intelligent one.

The one who can handle things. The one who keeps everything steady.

This identity is rewarding. It affirms her sense of self as capable, reliable, strong.

But it also makes it harder to step out of the role.

Because stepping out of it feels like becoming someone else.

The Shift She Couldn't Name

The change does not arrive dramatically.

At first, she feels competent. Then responsible. Then, gradually, alone in that responsibility.

What once felt like contribution begins to feel like obligation. What once felt like care begins to feel like maintenance.

Because the shift is gradual, it is difficult to name.

Silent Overextension

This is the stage most people miss.

Because she is still functioning. Still showing up. Still doing what needs to be done. Still keeping things intact.

But something has changed.

She is no longer giving freely. She is sustaining something.

And sustaining requires energy—energy that is not being replenished.

The First Signs

The signs are subtle.

Fatigue after conversations that once felt easy. Reluctance where there used to be enthusiasm. Irritation that seems out of proportion.

And a quiet thought that surfaces, then disappears:

Why is this always on me?

Why She Minimizes It

Even when she notices these feelings, she dismisses them.

Everyone has difficult phases. Relationships require effort. No one is perfect.

She tells herself she is being unfair. Too sensitive. Expecting too much.

And so she adjusts again.

The Loop That Forms

A loop takes shape.

She feels strain, questions herself, adjusts—and the relationship stabilizes, temporarily.

That stability reinforces the belief that her effort is what keeps things working.

So she continues.

The Loneliness of Strength

There is a particular loneliness in being the strong one.

Because strength is rarely supported. It is relied upon.

People assume you can handle things. That you need less. That you are less affected.

So they give less—not out of malice, but out of assumption.

What She Needed

She did not need perfection.

She needed reciprocity.

Effort that met her where she was. Responsibility that was shared. Care that was not contingent on her maintaining it.

But because she was used to being capable, she did not always recognize when those things were missing.

The Breaking Point

The woman who loved well does not break early.

She adapts. Continues. Endures longer than most.

Which is why, when she finally reaches her limit, it appears sudden.

But it is not.

It is cumulative.

Years of small imbalances. Quiet overextension. Being the one who held everything together.

What This Chapter Is Saying

This is not an argument against effort, or care, or generosity. These are essential to any meaningful relationship.

But they must be mutual. Balanced. Not resting on one person alone.

The Reframe

The woman who loved well was not the problem.

Her strength was not the problem. Her willingness to give was not the problem.

The problem was that her strength was unshared.

Her effort unbalanced.

Her love asked to carry more than it should have.

The Beginning of Clarity

Understanding this is not about blame.

It is about clarity.

So that she can recognize the pattern earlier. See it as it forms.

And step out of it before it defines the relationship.

The Final Truth

Love requires effort.

But it does not require one person to carry it. And it does not reward the one who gives the most.

The woman who loved well was not too much.

She was simply doing too much—for far too long.

Chapter 7

The Good Wife Script

Chapter 6 was about who she became. This chapter is about how she was trained to become her.

Young women are quietly trained to believe this:

- Being low-maintenance keeps him loyal.

- Agreeableness keeps him calm.

- Compromise keeps the relationship stable.

But none of those secure commitment. They only secure *access*.

The Pattern Was Installed Before It Was Chosen

The woman who loved well did not arrive at that way of loving on her own.

It was shaped over time, through repetition, reinforcement, and reward.

Not deliberately. Not through explicit instruction, but through a steady accumulation of signals about what made a woman desirable, acceptable, and easy to love.

By the time she entered a serious relationship, much of this pattern was already in place. It did not feel like something she had learned. It felt like something she simply knew.

The Script No One Names

No one presents it as a script.

There is no moment where she is told, clearly and directly, how she is expected to behave in order to be loved well. And yet, most women could recognize the pattern immediately.

Be agreeable.
Be emotionally controlled.
Be sexually available.
Do not be a drama queen.

Also:
Keep things running smoothly.
Keep the relationship stable.
Keep him comfortable.
Keep the peace.

These are not rules she consciously agreed to. They are expectations she absorbed, gradually, until they became instinct.

Why It Feels Like Maturity

The difficulty is that this script does not feel limiting. It feels advanced.

It sounds like emotional intelligence. Like self-awareness.

Like the kind of behavior that sustains long-term relationships.

After all, who wants to be difficult, reactive, or unnecessarily confrontational? Who wants to create tension where none is needed?

So she learns to regulate herself.

She learns to think before she speaks, to soften her tone, to present concerns in ways that are more likely to be received well.

These are valuable skills.

But when applied unevenly, when one person is doing most of the adjusting and most of the regulating, they begin to function less as maturity and more as maintenance.

Where It Begins

This pattern does not begin in adulthood. It starts much earlier, in subtle social feedback that teaches girls what is rewarded and what is penalized.

The agreeable girl is liked. The emotionally contained girl is praised. The girl who does not disrupt the group is included.

Over time, she learns that likeability is not just who she is, but how she behaves. She learns to monitor herself, to soften her reactions, to prioritize harmony over expression.

None of this is presented as compromise. It is framed as being easy to be around.

The Social Cost of Friction

Friction carries a cost.

Disagreement risks exclusion. Directness risks being labelled difficult. Strong emotion risks dismissal.

So she adapts.

She becomes more accommodating, more measured, more careful. She learns to manage her reactions before anyone else has to.

This becomes second nature. By the time she is an adult, it no longer feels like effort. It feels like who she is.

The Policing of Emotion

The "You're being dramatic/neurotic" accusation is one of the most effective ways to regulate a woman's behavior.

It does not engage with what she is saying. It reframes how she is saying it. It shifts the focus from the issue to her reaction.

If she is upset, the question becomes whether her reaction is appropriate, rather than whether the situation warranted it.

So she learns to calibrate herself. To present concerns calmly, to minimize intensity, to make her emotions easier to receive.

Even when what she is responding to has not been made easier for her.

Desire Without Demands

As she moves into adult relationships, the script evolves.

She is encouraged to be desirable, confident, and open. She is told to be comfortable with intimacy, to express desire, to reject shame.

But alongside this message sits another expectation, one that is less visible but equally influential.

That she should not make demands.

That she should not require too much reassurance, clarity, or effort.

She learns to balance herself carefully. To be appealing, but not inconvenient. To be wanted, but not difficult to keep.

Sexual Availability as Relationship Wisdom

This is where the script becomes more complex.

Modern relationship advice often presents sexual openness as a marker of maturity. It is framed as part of a healthy partnership:

"Keep the spark alive."

"Don't let things go cold."

"Physical connection matters."

All of this is true, in part. But beneath it sits a quieter implication, one that is rarely stated directly.

That maintaining sexual availability helps stabilize the relationship.

That responsiveness prevents distance.

That refusal, if it happens too often, introduces risk.

How It Is Internalized

These ideas are not experienced as pressure. They are experienced as understanding.

She does not feel forced. She feels informed.

So she incorporates them. She becomes attentive not just to her own desire, but to the state of the relationship—to what might sustain it, to what might weaken it.

And in doing so, intimacy begins to shift.

Not immediately. Not completely. But subtly.

From expression to maintenance.

The Maintenance Woman

She is not born. She is formed.

Not through explicit instruction, but through a series of quiet reinforcements about what it takes to be chosen, and more importantly, to remain chosen.

She learns that partnership is not simply entered into. It is earned, and then maintained. Not through presence alone, but through service. Through being agreeable, responsive, accommodating. Through making the relationship function smoothly enough that it never comes under threat.

In this framework, love is not something that stands on its own.

It is something that must be sustained.

Sex, within this model, is no longer understood purely as desire. It becomes part of that support system, something that helps stabilize the connection, something that reassures, something that prevents distance.

It is not described as obligation—but it is rarely treated as entirely free.

The Goal of Staying Partnered

Alongside this sits a deeper assumption, one that is rarely examined:

That staying partnered is the goal.

Not being well within the relationship. Not being met fully. Not being in something that is genuinely mutual.

But *staying*.

And when staying becomes the priority, standards shift.

Staying Partnered at All Costs Lowers Standards

What is tolerated expands. What is expected begins to contract. What once might have been questioned becomes something to work around.

This is how the maintenance mindset takes hold.

Not as a conscious strategy, but as a way of being that feels responsible, mature, even loving.

She becomes the woman who keeps things going.

The woman who adjusts.

The woman who ensures that nothing breaks.

And because she does it well, it is rarely questioned.

It is praised. It is called *commitment*.

But what is being maintained, and at what cost, is a question that comes later.

Much later.

The Emotional Climate

Alongside sexual responsiveness, there is another expectation that is even less visible.

She becomes responsible, in some quiet way, for the emotional climate.

She notices when things feel off. She intervenes early. She smooths tension before it becomes conflict.

She keeps things manageable.

This is rarely articulated, but it is widely modelled.

In the stories she has seen and absorbed, women are often the ones who hold the emotional centre.

They are not described as overburdened. They are described as strong.

Cultural Reinforcement

The script is reinforced everywhere.

In families, where women often manage emotional continuity.

In culture, where women who endure and adapt are praised.

In media, where the ideal partner is both independent and easy to be with, strong but accommodating, confident but not demanding.

These contradictions are not resolved externally—they are managed internally.

By her.

The Cost of Being Perfect

In the series, *Mad Men,* perfect wife Betty Draper sits in immaculate rooms, perfectly dressed, perfectly composed, living a life that appears effortless from the outside.

She is beautiful, controlled, desirable in the way she has been taught to be.

And yet, there is a persistent unease beneath the surface.

Her role is clear. Be agreeable. Be composed. Be desirable—but not difficult. Maintain the atmosphere. Do not disrupt what appears to be working.

What makes her compelling is not her perfection, but the strain of maintaining it.

The sense that her life is something she is performing rather than inhabiting.

Competence Mistaken for Intimacy

The result of this conditioning is a woman who is highly competent in relationships.

She communicates clearly. She regulates her emotions. She anticipates needs. She maintains connection.

From the outside, this looks like intimacy. The relationship appears smooth, stable, and functional.

But competence is not intimacy. It only looks like it.

Competence is management.

The Illusion of Closeness

Intimacy requires mutual engagement, mutual effort, mutual responsibility.

But when one person is doing most of the adjusting, most of the maintaining, most of the regulating, the relationship can feel close while being structurally unequal.

It works—but only because one person is holding it together.

This is difficult to see, because the outcome, at least initially, is positive. There is less conflict, less disruption, more continuity.

She believes she is doing relationships well.

And in one sense, she is.

Why It Holds

The system works.

When she adjusts, tension decreases. When she smooths things over, connection returns. When she gives more, the relationship stabilizes.

So the behavior is reinforced.

Not because it is sustainable, but because it produces immediate results.

The Cost Appears Later

Over time, the imbalance becomes harder to ignore.

She begins to notice how often she is the one adjusting, anticipating, maintaining.

She begins to feel the effort more clearly.

But by then, the pattern is established.

And patterns, once established, are difficult to disrupt.

The Reframe

The shift she eventually makes is subtle but significant.

From believing she is naturally good at relationships—to recognizing that she has been trained to carry them.

What This Chapter Is Asking You to See

Not that you are too accommodating.

Not that you are too generous.

But that these traits were shaped, reinforced, and rewarded.

That they were not simply personal.

They were patterned.

The Quiet Truth

You were not simply being yourself.

You were following a script that made you effective, desirable, and easy to be with.

But not necessarily *equal.*

What Changes Once You See It

Once the script becomes visible, it is difficult to ignore.

You begin to notice the instinct to smooth, the impulse to adjust, the reflex to maintain.

And you begin to question them.

Not with guilt, but with curiosity.

The Question That Interrupts the Pattern

Not how to make the relationship work better.

But why it depends on you to make it work at all.

The Final Line

You were not wrong to learn how to love well.

You were merely taught to do it alone.

Chapter 8

Emotional Infrastructure

She did not decide to become responsible for the emotional life of the relationship.

It happened gradually, through small, reasonable responses to things that needed attention.

There was no single moment where she took on the role, no conversation in which it was assigned.

Instead, it emerged through repetition, through habit, through the quiet logic of who notices—and who responds.

Over time, she became the one who noticed.

The Relationship's Nervous System

Every relationship has a nervous system—something that detects shifts in tone, registers tension, and responds to emotional changes.

In a balanced dynamic, this system is shared. Both people notice when something is off, both respond, and both take responsibility for restoring connection.

But in many relationships, that responsibility consolidates. It becomes centered in one person.

And very often, that person is her.

She feels the shift before it is spoken. A slight withdrawal, a change in tone, a distance that has not yet been named. Something is different, and she senses it almost immediately.

This sensitivity is not a flaw. It is a form of awareness. But awareness, when it is not shared, quickly becomes responsibility.

Mood Management

At first, she simply pays attention. Then she begins to adjust.

If he is quiet, she softens her approach. If he is stressed, she becomes more accommodating. If he is irritable, she becomes more careful with her tone.

She modulates herself in response to him—not dramatically, not always consciously, but consistently.

She learns his moods—what unsettles him, what reassures him, what helps him return to equilibrium.

She begins to anticipate his emotional state and to act accordingly.

Over time, this becomes automatic. She is no longer just present in the relationship, she is regulating it.

The Work of Keeping Things Steady

What she is doing is subtle—but it is not small.

She is maintaining the emotional weather of the relationship. She is preventing escalation, smoothing tension before it hardens into conflict, and keeping the atmosphere liveable.

Because she does this well, the relationship appears stable. There are fewer arguments, fewer disruptions, fewer visible fractures.

From the outside, it works.

What is less visible is that this stability is being actively maintained—and that she is the one maintaining it.

Conflict Buffering

When conflict arises, she does not ignore it, but she handles it carefully.

She chooses her words. She considers timing. She anticipates how something will be received before she says it. She edits herself in real time—softening edges, removing anything that might escalate.

If tension increases, she de-escalates. If he withdraws, she reaches. If something remains unresolved, she reintroduces it, gently, in a way that might be easier to receive.

She becomes skilled at navigating conflict without letting it destabilize the relationship.

This skill is valuable, but it is not neutral. It requires attention, energy, and restraint. And when it is not shared, it becomes a form of labor.

Translating His Emotions

There is another layer to this role, one that is rarely named.

She becomes an interpreter.

He may not always articulate what he is feeling, but she can sense it. She reads the pauses, the tone shifts, the small changes in behavior that signal something beneath the surface.

And so she gives it language.

She names what he cannot quite express. She offers interpretations, helps him process, helps him understand himself.

This can feel like intimacy. Like closeness. Like a deep form of connection where one person is attuned enough to meet the other where they are.

But over time, something changes.

She is no longer just sharing emotional space. She is structuring it.

The Asymmetry That Forms

The more she takes on this role, the less he has to.

Not because he chooses not to, but because the system has adapted. If she is the one who notices, names, and resolves, then those functions are already being handled.

There is no gap left for him to step into.

And so the relationship begins to organize itself around her competence.

She becomes the one who monitors, who initiates, who repairs. He becomes the one who responds within the environment she creates.

This arrangement is not discussed—but it is real.

The Expansion of Responsibility

Her role expands quietly.

She is now responsible for noticing emotional shifts, initiating conversations, maintaining connection, translating unspoken feelings, and preventing escalation before it begins.

None of this was assigned. None of it explicitly agreed upon.

But all of it now rests with her.

She is no longer just participating in the relationship. She is maintaining its emotional continuity.

Why She Continues

She continues because it works.

When she intervenes early, tension dissolves. When she names what is happening, it becomes manageable. When she smooths things over, the relationship returns to equilibrium.

The immediate outcome is positive—and so the behavior is reinforced.

The alternative, allowing things to sit unresolved, allowing distance to grow, allowing conflict to remain uncontained, feels riskier.

So she tells herself it is easier this way.

The Beginning of Resentment

Resentment does not begin with anger. It begins with imbalance.

With the quiet awareness that one person is doing more. More noticing. More adjusting. More carrying.

At first, this awareness is fleeting. A moment of irritation, a thought that passes quickly.

Why is this always on me?

She does not dwell on it. She minimizes it, reframes it, reminds herself that relationships require effort, that no one is perfect, that this is normal.

And so she continues.

Invisible Labor

What makes this stage particularly difficult is that the work she is doing is largely invisible.

It does not appear as a task. It has no clear boundary. It cannot be easily measured or divided.

But it is work.

The work of attention, regulation, anticipation, and repair. The work of maintaining emotional continuity so that the relationship feels intact.

Because it is invisible, it is rarely acknowledged. And because it is rarely acknowledged, it is rarely shared.

The Body Registers What the Mind Minimizes

Even when she does not consciously name the imbalance, her body registers it.

There is a growing fatigue. A tension that was not there before. A subtle resistance where there used to be ease.

She may not articulate it clearly, but she feels it.

Something has become heavier.

From Willingness to Responsibility

At the beginning, she chooses to care. Later, she becomes responsible for caring.

This is the shift.

If she does not notice, who will? If she does not address it, who will bring things back into balance?

Her role has become essential.

And essential roles are difficult to step away from.

Why It Is Hard to Stop

By the time she recognizes the pattern, it is already established.

If she withdraws, something changes. The relationship feels less stable, less connected, more uncertain.

Stepping back does not feel like relief. It feels like risk.

And so she continues, even as the cost becomes more apparent.

The Trap of Emotional Competence

Her strength is what created this dynamic.

Her awareness, her emotional intelligence, her ability to regulate and respond, all of these qualities made her effective.

But they also made her responsible.

Because she could do it, she did. And because she did, it became hers.

The Unspoken Contract

Without ever being articulated, a contract has formed.

She will maintain the emotional integrity of the relationship. He will respond within it.

This is not malicious. It is not even conscious.

But it is unequal.

The Moment of Clarity

Eventually, she begins to see it.

Not all at once, but in moments.

Moments where she notices how quickly she moves to restore balance, how instinctively she absorbs tension, how automatically she takes responsibility for what is happening between them.

And something in her pauses.

What This Chapter Is Asking You to See

A relationship should not rely on one person to detect, regulate, and repair its emotional life.

It should not require one person to hold everything together.

Because when one person becomes the emotional infrastructure, they stop being free within the relationship.

They become responsible for it.

The First Shift

The goal is not to care less.

It is to stop carrying it alone.

But before that can happen, she has to see what she has been doing.

The Resenting

Resentment does not begin when things fall apart.

It begins when one person has been holding everything together—quietly, consistently—for far too long.

Chapter 9

THE COMPETENCE TRAP

She did not become indispensable by accident. She became indispensable because she was capable.

Competence is one of the most attractive qualities a person can have. It signals stability, reliability, and maturity.

A competent woman can organize a life. She plans, anticipates, and executes. She does not create chaos; she contains it.

In the early stages of a relationship, this is deeply appealing. She makes things easier. Smoother. More functional. Plans come together without friction. Details are handled. Nothing is forgotten.

She books the restaurant, remembers the dates, coordinates the plans. Not because she has to, but because she can—and because it feels natural.

What is not immediately visible is that competence, once demonstrated, rarely remains optional. It becomes expected.

When Capability Becomes the Default

In any relationship, patterns form not through agreement but through repetition. The person who does something well tends to keep doing it. Over time, that behavior becomes their role.

If she plans effectively, she becomes the planner. If she organizes without error, she becomes the organizer. If she handles things without fuss, she becomes the one who handles them.

No one assigns these roles. They emerge quietly, and once they emerge, they tend to persist.

What begins as contribution gradually becomes default.

The Shift Toward Dependence

At first, the arrangement feels balanced. She does more in certain areas, he contributes in others, and the relationship appears to function well.

But competence has a gravitational pull. It draws responsibility toward it.

If she handles logistics smoothly, there is little pressure for him to develop that skill. If she anticipates needs before they arise, there is no gap for him to notice. If she keeps track of details, there is no consequence for him overlooking them.

The system adjusts, not out of intention, but out of efficiency.

And over time, the balance begins to tilt.

The Emergence of Passive Incompetence

In some relationships, this shift becomes more pronounced. What begins as passivity evolves into a kind of learned helplessness.

He does not know how. He is not good at that. He will probably get it wrong.

So she does it.

Not because she wants to take on more, but because it is easier than correcting him, faster than waiting, and more reliable than leaving things undone.

This dynamic is sometimes described as *weaponized helplessness*, but it does not always feel deliberate. More often, it presents as a pattern of avoidance that is quietly reinforced by her willingness to compensate.

The outcome, however, is the same. She carries more.

The Expansion of Invisible Work
The shift is not dramatic. It accumulates.

What begins with small acts of organization expands into a broader responsibility for the logistics of shared life.

She keeps track of schedules, appointments, social obligations, and household needs. She remembers what must be done and when. She anticipates what will be required next.

She becomes, without ever being formally assigned the role, the operational center of the relationship.

And because much of this work is invisible, it is rarely acknowledged.

The Efficiency Illusion
She becomes highly efficient. She can manage multiple layers of responsibility with minimal disruption. She keeps things running.

From the outside, this looks like success. The relationship appears stable, organized, and functional.

But efficiency has a cost.

The smoother she makes things, the less visible her effort becomes. And the less visible it becomes, the more it is taken for granted.

What was once appreciated becomes assumed.

From Partner to Function

At a certain point, something shifts in how she is experienced.

She is no longer just a partner. She becomes a function.

A system of reliability. A source of continuity. The person who ensures that life proceeds without interruption.

This makes her indispensable.

But it also changes the nature of her value.

Indispensable Is Not the Same as Desired

There is a fundamental difference between being needed and being wanted.

Need is tied to function. It's about what you provide, what you manage, what would be missed if you were no longer there.

Desire is different. It's not about utility. It is about presence, attraction, and choice.

When a woman becomes indispensable, she risks being valued primarily for what she does rather than for who she is.

And while usefulness can sustain a life, it does not sustain desire.

Why Usefulness Erodes Polarity

Romantic attraction depends, in part, on contrast. On a sense of difference that creates curiosity and engagement.

But when one person becomes the organizer, the manager, the stabilizer, they move into a role defined by responsibility rather than presence.

She becomes predictable. Reliable. Always there, always capable.

These are admirable qualities, but they do not generate tension or intrigue. They do not invite pursuit.

Over time, she is not experienced as someone to be discovered, but as someone to be depended on.

The Subtle Change in His Orientation

As her role becomes more functional, his orientation toward her shifts.

He relies on her. He expects her. He assumes continuity.

This is not necessarily a loss of care—it is a change in posture.

Expectation begins to replace appreciation.

And expectation, once established, rarely feels like admiration.

Why She Continues

She continues because it works.

Because things get done. Because life runs more smoothly when she is managing it. Because stepping back introduces friction—and friction feels like failure.

If she does less, things are forgotten. Plans fall through. Details are missed.

So she compensates.

Not out of obligation, but out of habit.

The Hidden Trade-Off

What she gains in stability, she loses in reciprocity.

What she gains in control, she loses in shared responsibility.

What she gains in being needed, she risks losing in being desired.

This trade-off is rarely explicit, but it is deeply consequential.

The Moment of Recognition

The realization does not arrive dramatically. It appears in small moments.

She notices she is doing more, planning more, remembering more, holding more.

And that this effort is not being matched.

At first, it's only an observation. Then it becomes a question.

And eventually, it becomes a pattern she can no longer ignore.

Why It Is Difficult to Reverse

By the time she sees it clearly, the dynamic is already established.

He is accustomed to her competence. She is accustomed to compensating.

If she steps back, there is disruption. The system no longer runs as smoothly.

And that disruption feels uncomfortable.

Not just for him, but for her.

The Fear Beneath the Pattern

If she stops doing everything, what happens?

Will he step forward, or will things fall apart?

Will the relationship rebalance—or degrade?

This uncertainty keeps her in place.

The Deeper Issue

The issue is not that she is capable.

The issue is that her capability has become the structure the relationship depends on.

Instead of two people contributing, one person compensates.

And compensation, sustained over time, becomes burden.

The Return of Resentment

As in emotional labor, resentment does not begin as anger. It begins as awareness.

She sees the imbalance. She feels the asymmetry. She recognizes how much rests on her.

And once she sees it, it becomes increasingly difficult to continue without questioning it.

A Necessary Reframe

Competence is not the problem.

Over-functioning is.

And over-functioning is not love. It is adaptation to an imbalance that has not been addressed.

The Question That Changes Everything

The question is no longer: "How can I do this better?"

It becomes:

"Why am I the one doing this at all?"

The Final Truth – Feeling More Alone

Being indispensable can keep a life running, but it cannot create an equal relationship.

And it cannot sustain desire.

Because the more she becomes the one who holds everything together, the less he has to.

And the more she carries, the more alone she becomes within the partnership.

Chapter 10

Death by Accommodation

Resentment rarely begins with something large enough to name.

It does not arrive with a clear cause, a single argument, or a moment that can be pointed to and explained. It does not begin with betrayal or obvious neglect.

It begins quietly.

With small decisions. Small adjustments. Small moments where something could have been said, and wasn't.

The Nature of Accommodation

Accommodation, in itself, is not a problem.

All relationships require it. People adjust to one another, make space, compromise when necessary. Without some degree of flexibility, no relationship could sustain itself over time.

But there is a difference between mutual accommodation and unilateral adjustment.

The difference between choosing to meet someone halfway and gradually moving the entire center of the relationship toward them.

That difference is rarely visible at the beginning.

Because it does not happen all at once.

The Micro-Compromises

It happens through what might be called micro-compromises.

Small, almost invisible moments where she adjusts herself to keep things smooth.

The cancelled plan that she pretends does not matter.

The comment she decides not to make because it might create tension.

The preference she sets aside because it seems easier than negotiating it.

Each decision is minor. Each one, on its own, is reasonable.

None of them feel like sacrifice.

Slow Erosion Without Rupture

There is a moment in the film *Revolutionary Road,* based on the novel by Richard Yates, where April Wheeler sits across from her husband, both of them still performing the version of their life that once felt full of promise.

Nothing has collapsed. They are still married, still functioning, still speaking in the language of a couple who should be fine.

And yet, something has already gone.

What is most striking is not the conflict—but the performance.

The way they continue to move through roles that no longer fit, saying things that no longer feel true, maintaining a version of the relationship that exists more in appearance than in experience.

This is how accommodation works at its most advanced stage.

Not as sacrifice. But as continuation.

The Logic of Letting It Go

In each moment, the reasoning is sound.

It's not worth making an issue of this.
He's tired.
It's been a long day.
I can let this one go.

She is not suppressing herself out of fear. She is making what feels like a mature choice. She is prioritising harmony over friction.

And because the immediate outcome is positive, the pattern reinforces itself.

The moment passes. The relationship remains intact.

The Accumulation

Patterns are not built from single moments. They are built from repetition.

What happens occasionally becomes what happens often. What happens often becomes what is expected.

Over time, the micro-compromises accumulate.

The cancelled plans are no longer occasional. The swallowed comments become habitual. The small preferences she set aside become part of a larger pattern of deference.

Nothing dramatic has occurred.

And yet, something has shifted.

What Goes Unsaid

The things she does not say do not disappear.

They remain—unexpressed but present—shaping how she experiences the relationship.

Not as a list of grievances, but as a quiet sense that something is not quite aligned.

She cannot always articulate it. There is no single incident to point to.

But there is a feeling.

A subtle imbalance.

The Apology She Didn't Owe

Sometimes, the shift becomes visible in language.

She apologizes when she has not done anything wrong.

For bringing something up.
For being upset.
For asking for clarity.

The apology is not always explicit. Sometimes it is embedded in tone, in how she softens what she says, in how she pre-emptively minimizes her own position.

"I know this might sound silly, but..."

"I don't want to make a big deal out of this..."

She reduces the weight of what she is saying before it can be dismissed.

The Gradual Recalibration

Over time, she recalibrates herself.

She becomes less likely to raise things that might disrupt the flow of the relationship. Less likely to insist on preferences that are not immediately accommodated.

Not because she has no preferences, but because expressing them feels increasingly costly.

Friction is avoided. Smoothness is prioritized.

And the relationship, on the surface, continues to function.

Why It Feels Like Maturity

This pattern is often mistaken for growth.

She is more patient. More measured. Less reactive.

She does not escalate unnecessarily. She does not turn every issue into a conflict.

These are, in isolation, positive traits.

But when they are not matched, they create an imbalance that is difficult to detect and even harder to address.

The Shift in Internal Experience
Externally, very little changes.

Internally, something does.

She begins to feel less spontaneous, less expressive, less fully herself.

There is a slight hesitation before she speaks. A calculation about whether something is worth saying.

A quiet editing process that runs continuously.

The Loss of Ease
What disappears first is ease.

Not dramatically, but gradually.

Conversations require more thought. Reactions are more controlled. There is less freedom to move through the relationship without consideration of how things will be received.

She becomes careful.

And care, when it is constant, becomes effort.

The Invisible Ledger

Even when she tells herself she is not keeping score, something in her is registering the imbalance.

Not as a conscious tally, but as a felt sense of giving more than she receives.

She notices how often she adjusts, how often she lets things go, how often she chooses harmony over honesty.

And although she does not always dwell on it, the awareness remains.

Why It Is Difficult to Interrupt

The pattern is difficult to interrupt because each individual moment is small.

There is no clear justification for changing course. No obvious point at which she can say, "This is where it went wrong."

It did not go wrong in one place.

It shifted everywhere, slowly.

The Reinforcement Loop

The loop continues.

She accommodates, the relationship stabilizes, and that stability reinforces the behavior.

Because it works in the short term, it is repeated.

And because it is repeated, it becomes the structure of the relationship.

The Cost of Constant Adjustment

Over time, the cost becomes more apparent.

Not as a single breaking point, but as a growing sense of depletion.

She feels more tired. More irritable. Less engaged.

Things that once felt easy now require effort.

Things that once felt natural now feel managed.

The First Clear Thought

At some point, the thought becomes more defined.

Not just a passing irritation, but a recognizable question.

Why am I always the one adjusting?

It does not always arrive with anger. Often it arrives with confusion.

A sense that something has shifted, but without a clear explanation of how.

Why She Still Minimizes It

Even then, she may minimize it.

Relationships are not perfect. Everyone compromises. This is what being an adult looks like.

She tells herself she is overthinking it.

And so the pattern continues.

The Emotional Consequence

What begins as accommodation becomes, over time, a quiet form of self-abandonment.

Not in a dramatic or visible way—but in a series of small decisions where she consistently chooses the relationship over her own immediate experience.

She does not disappear all at once.

She recedes—gradually.

The Emergence of Resentment

Resentment does not announce itself.

It forms beneath the surface, shaped by repeated moments of unexpressed dissatisfaction.

It is not tied to one event, but to many.

Many small concessions. Many quiet adjustments. Many times she chose not to say what she really thought or felt.

Why It Feels Confusing

When resentment finally becomes visible, it often feels disproportionate.

The relationship may look stable. There may be no obvious reason for the intensity of what she is feeling.

But the feeling is not coming from one moment.

It is coming from accumulation.

The Name for What Happened

Nothing dramatic occurred.

There was no single failure.

Just a slow, consistent pattern of accommodation that shifted the relationship, one small moment at a time.

The Reframe

Accommodating others is not inherently harmful.

But when it is not mutual, when one person consistently adjusts more than the other, it becomes something else.

It becomes erosion.

The Question That Matters

Not: "Is this a big enough issue to raise?"

But: "Why am I the one deciding that it isn't?"

The Final Truth

Resentment does not begin with something large enough to confront.

It begins with things too small to justify addressing.

And it grows, quietly and steadily, until it is no longer small at all.

Chapter 11

Sᴇx ᴀs Iɴsᴜʀᴀɴᴄᴇ

Sex in long term relationships did not begin as obligation.

If it did, most women would recognize it immediately. They would resist it, question it, probably refuse it.

Instead, it begins as something far more reasonable.

Something that feels like care.

The Desire to Keep Things Good

In the early stages of a relationship, intimacy is not complicated.

It is spontaneous, mutual, connected to genuine desire. It feels like an extension of closeness rather than something separate.

But as the relationship settles, intimacy begins to carry more meaning.

It becomes, quietly, a signal.
That things are still good.
That connection is intact.

That nothing important has been lost.

She may not articulate it this way, but she feels it.

The First Adjustment

There is a moment, often small enough to go unnoticed, when she is not entirely in the mood.

She is tired. Distracted. Not fully present.

He reaches for her, she hesitates, briefly. And then she says yes.

Not out of pressure. Not out of fear. But out of a subtle calculation that happens almost instantly.

It will be easier.
It will be nice for him.
It will keep things close.

It feels like kindness.

Why It Feels Harmless

Because it is, at first.

She still enjoys it most of the time. She still feels connected. There is no sense of violation, no clear boundary crossed.

It is simply a moment where her desire is not the primary driver.

And that, in itself, does not seem significant.

The Shift in Meaning

But something has changed.

Intimacy is no longer only about expression. It is also about maintenance.

About keeping the relationship in a good state. About preventing distance before it forms.

She is not just responding to her own desire. She is responding to the condition of the relationship.

The Logic of Prevention

The reasoning is quiet, but consistent.

If intimacy slows down, things might drift.

If he feels rejected too often, he might withdraw.

If he withdraws, connection becomes harder to restore.

So she stays ahead of it. She prevents the distance rather than addressing it later.

Reassurance Disguised as Intimacy

Over time, intimacy becomes a form of reassurance.

Reassuring him.
The relationship.
Herself that everything is still intact.

She does not think of this as a strategy. It feels instinctive, almost automatic.

But the function has shifted.

The Subtle Humiliation

There is a particular feeling that emerges here, one that is difficult to name.

It is not resentment, not yet. It is not even discomfort in the usual sense.

It is something quieter.

A faint awareness that she is participating in something she does not fully want—for a reason she does not fully examine.

A sense of performing—even if only slightly.

She may not dwell on it.

She may not even consciously acknowledge it.

But it registers.

The Body Knows Before the Mind Does

Her body begins to respond differently.

Not dramatically, but subtly.

A slight lack of enthusiasm. A delay in responsiveness. A sense of moving through it rather than into it.

She tells herself it is nothing. Everyone feels this way sometimes.

And she is not wrong.

But what matters is not the individual moment.

It is the pattern.

The Pattern Strengthens

It happens again.

And then again.

Not constantly, not every time—but often enough to become familiar.

She says yes when she is tired. Yes when she would have preferred rest. Yes when she senses that it will make things easier.

Each time, it feels small.

Each time, it seems harmless.

Why She Doesn't Question It

Because it works.

Connection is maintained. Tension is avoided. The relationship continues to feel stable.

There is no immediate cost.

And so there is no reason, yet, to interrogate the pattern.

The Unspoken Exchange

Occasionally, the shift becomes more visible.

In a comment. A tone. A joke that carries more meaning than it appears to.

"I guess I'm doing something right."
"I'm glad you're in a good mood tonight."

Or more explicitly: "I took care of things earlier."

The language is light—but the implication is not.

Intimacy is beginning to register as something that influences the relationship's equilibrium.

When Intimacy Becomes Strategic

She does not want to think of it this way, but she begins to notice that intimacy has effects beyond itself.

It improves the atmosphere. It softens tension. It restores closeness.

And so, gradually, it becomes something she uses.

Not manipulatively—functionally.

The Cost of Using It

What she gains in stability, she begins to lose in spontaneity.

Desire becomes less central. Awareness becomes more so.

She is thinking about the impact of intimacy, not just experiencing it.

And thinking is not the same as wanting.

The Quiet Erosion

This is where the erosion begins.

Not of the relationship, but of her relationship to her *own desire.*

Because each time she overrides it—even slightly—something shifts.

Desire becomes less reliable. Less immediate. Less trusted.

The Internal Split

A subtle division forms.

What she feels.
What she chooses.

They are no longer always aligned.

And while the gap is small, it is growing.

Why It Matters

Because desire depends on freedom.

On the ability to want without obligation, to respond without calculation, to engage without purpose beyond itself.

Once it begins to serve another function, it changes.

Not all at once.

But steadily.

The Moment She Notices

At some point, she becomes aware of it.

Not as a theory, but as a feeling.

A moment where she realizes she is not entirely present.

That she is participating—but not fully wanting.

And the question surfaces:

When did this start to feel like something I do—rather than something I want?

The Reframe

This is not about blame.

Not about him, and not about her.

It is about recognising the shift in function.

Intimacy has moved from expression to maintenance.

From desire to reassurance.

What This Chapter Is Asking You to See

Not that occasional compromise is wrong.

But that repeated, unexamined compromise creates a pattern.

And that pattern, over time, changes how desire is experienced.

The Final Truth

Sex does not become obligation all at once.

It becomes insurance first.

And anything used to secure a relationship eventually stops being free.

Chapter 12

And So She Tries

She tries to be open-minded about sex.

She tries not to be prudish, guarded, or overly cautious.

She wants to appear mature and relaxed about desire, not anxious or withholding.

Sex, after all, is supposed to be natural.

And so she learns early on that sexual generosity is not just about pleasure.

It is also about stability.

If she is enthusiastic enough, the thinking goes, he will feel satisfied. If he feels satisfied, he will stay emotionally close. If he stays emotionally close, the relationship will feel safe.

This idea is so common it barely registers at all. It feels like common sense.

But embedded within it is a quiet shift: sex stops being only an expression of desire and begins to function as something else.

A reassurance. A peace offering. An invisible form of maintenance.

At twenty-five, this seems harmless.

At thirty-five, many women begin to feel its weight.

By forty-five, many can see the pattern with painful clarity.

They were not just lovers. They had become managers of emotional stability.

None of this felt manipulative at the time.

She did not think of herself as performing. She thought she was being loving.

If he seemed distant, she leaned closer. If he was stressed, she softened the evening. If there had been tension earlier in the day, she might initiate intimacy at night, hoping the warmth would dissolve the tension.

These gestures were sincere. But sincerity does not prevent exhaustion.

Over time, something subtle begins to happen.

Her generosity becomes expected. Her emotional labour becomes invisible.

And what she once offered freely begins to feel less like love and more like obligation attached to the role she now occupies.

Girlfriend.

Partner.

Wife.

None of these roles arrive with an official job description. Yet almost every woman who has inhabited them long enough recognizes the duties.

Keep the relationship emotionally stable. Keep communication flowing. Keep intimacy alive. Keep the peace.

She does not remember formally accepting these responsibilities. They accumulated around her over the years until they felt inseparable from the relationship itself.

When intimacy faltered, she felt responsible for reviving it. When conflict lingered, responsible for resolving it. When emotional distance crept in, responsible for closing it.

He may have loved her. He may even have respected her.

But she had quietly become the nervous system of the relationship.

And nervous systems do not get days off.

Chapter 13

The Slow Slide

The resentment years rarely begin with anger.

They begin with fatigue.

Fatigue from being the one who notices everything. From initiating difficult conversations. From keeping track of anniversaries, family obligations, emotional undercurrents.

Fatigue from being the one who asks, gently but persistently, for the relationship to be tended to.

At first she tells herself that this imbalance is temporary. Every couple goes through phases. He will step up once things settle down.

Months pass. Years pass. The pattern remains.

And somewhere deep in her body, something begins to shift.

It is not yet rage. Not yet contempt.

It is the first quiet awareness that the love she offered so freely has turned into work she now performs.

The Invisible Contract

This book is not about blaming men. Nor is it about shaming women.

It is about examining the invisible contract that many women enter without realising it exists.

A contract that tells them their devotion will secure stability. That their emotional labor will be reciprocated. That if they are generous enough—patient enough, loving enough, sexually available enough—the relationship will remain safe.

For some couples, this belief works well enough.

For many others, it slowly erodes the woman who believed in it.

Years later, when the marriage finally fractures—or when she finally leaves—the outside world often asks the same puzzled question. What happened?

From the outside, it looked stable. There were no spectacular betrayals. No obvious disasters. Just two people who gradually stopped being happy together.

But inside the relationship, the story was different.

Inside the relationship, there had been years of small concessions. Emotional over-functioning. Trying to hold the center steady.

Years in which desire slowly became duty.

Those were the resentment years.

And they did not begin with resentment at all.

They began with love.

The Slow Slide

There is no moment where she can say, with certainty, that everything changed.

No single decision that altered the course of the relationship. No clear point at which what was once mutual became something she carried alone.

Instead, there is a slide—

Gradual, almost imperceptible, made up of small adjustments that, at the time, feel reasonable.

If she were asked when it began, she would struggle to answer.

Because nothing, on its own, seemed significant enough to mark.

How It Happens Without Notice

The slow slide is not a failure of awareness. It is a feature of how the pattern develops.

Each change is minor. Each adjustment makes sense. Each compromise feels temporary, necessary, or simply easier than the alternative.

There is no moment that demands attention.

And so attention is not given.

You Did More Because You Cared More

At the centre of this shift is something that feels, at first, like a strength.

She cares.

She cares about the relationship—how it feels, whether it is working. She is invested in its success, in its continuity, in the possibility of building something that lasts.

And because she cares, she does more.

She notices what needs attention and attends to it. She sees where things could improve and she moves toward that improvement. She senses distance and she closes it.

None of this feels like sacrifice.

It feels like love.

But caring more does not remain neutral.

Over time, it becomes effort. And when effort is not matched, it becomes imbalance.

The Quiet Logic of Adjustment

When something feels slightly off, she responds.

If communication is strained, she communicates more clearly.

If connection feels distant, she becomes more attentive. If tension emerges, she softens her approach.

She does not wait for things to deteriorate. She intervenes early, in small ways, to keep the relationship steady.

This feels like maturity.

Like taking responsibility.

Like doing what is necessary to maintain something important.

You Made Excuses Because You Were Loyal

Loyalty plays a particular role in the slow slide.

It encourages interpretation.

She does not take every moment at face value. She contextualizes. Explains. Looks for reasons that make his behavior understandable.

He's stressed.
He didn't mean it that way.
He's just not good at expressing himself.

These explanations are not always wrong. Often, they are accurate.

But they serve a function beyond understanding.

They soften the impact.

They make it easier to stay.

The Benefit of the Doubt

Giving someone the benefit of the doubt is often framed as generosity.

And it can be.

But when it becomes habitual, it can also obscure patterns.

Individual moments are explained away before they can accumulate into something meaningful. Each instance is treated as separate, rather than as part of a larger dynamic.

And so the pattern remains difficult to see.

"Every Relationship Has Issues"

There is another belief that sustains the slide.

Every relationship has issues.

This is true. No relationship is without tension, without difference, without moments of strain. Expecting perfection is unrealistic.

So when something feels off, she normalizes it.

This is just part of being in a relationship.
No one has it easy all the time.
This is what commitment looks like.

These thoughts are not irrational. They are grounded in reality.

But they also create a wide tolerance for imbalance.

The Expansion of Tolerance
Over time, her threshold shifts.

What would once have stood out begins to feel familiar. What would once have prompted a conversation becomes something she absorbs.

She becomes more accommodating, not because she has no limits, but because her limits have moved.

Gradually, without clear intention, she becomes someone who can tolerate more.

Why Nothing Feels Urgent
One of the most deceptive aspects of the slow slide is that nothing feels urgent.

There is no crisis. No dramatic rupture. No moment that demands immediate action.

The relationship continues.

It functions.

There are still good moments, still connection, still reasons to stay.

And so the underlying shift remains unaddressed.

The Accumulation of Small Imbalances
What is happening is not one large imbalance, but many small ones.

She initiates more. She adjusts more. She carries more.

Not in obvious ways, but in consistent ones.

Each imbalance, on its own, is manageable.

Together, they create a pattern.

The Loss of Reciprocity

At some point, she begins to notice something difficult to articulate.

Not that he does nothing, but that he does less.

Less noticing, less initiating, less adjusting.

The relationship still exists, but the effort required to sustain it is no longer evenly distributed.

The Erosion of Mutuality

In the mini-series *Scenes from a Marriage*, there is no single moment where the relationship breaks.

Instead, there is a gradual exposure.

Conversations that reveal more than they resolve. Small imbalances that become visible over time. A growing awareness that what exists between them is no longer what it once was.

What makes it difficult to watch is not the conflict, but the recognition.

The sense that nothing dramatic caused this, and yet everything has changed.

This is how the slow slide unfolds.

Not through collapse—but through accumulation.

Why She Doesn't Name It

Naming it would require confronting it.

And confronting it introduces risk.

If she says something, it may create tension. If she pushes, it may lead to conflict. If she insists, it may reveal something she is not ready to face.

So she waits. She gives it time.

She assumes it will rebalance.

The Role of Hope

Hope sustains the slow slide.

The belief that things will improve, that this is a phase, that the relationship will return to what it was.

She remembers how it felt at the beginning. The ease. The mutuality. The sense that both were equally invested.

She assumes that version still exists.

It just needs to be reached again.

The Effort to Return

And so she tries.

Not dramatically, but persistently.

She communicates more clearly. Becomes more attentive. Gives the relationship the benefit of her effort.

She believes, often sincerely, that if she does this well enough, things will return to balance.

The Subtle Realization

Over time, something begins to shift in her perception.

She notices that the effort is not temporary.

That it does not reduce once things stabilize.

That she is not restoring balance—but maintaining it.

The Question That Emerges

The question does not arrive loudly. It appears quietly, in moments of pause.

When did this become something I have to manage?

It is not yet an accusation.

It is an observation.

Why It Takes So Long to See

The slow slide is difficult to recognize because it never presents itself as a single problem.

It is a series of small, reasonable decisions that, over time, produce an unreasonable outcome.

Each step is logical.

The pattern is not.

The Cost of Staying Unaware

By the time she sees it clearly, the dynamic is already established.

The roles are set. The expectations are formed. The imbalance is no longer occasional, but structural.

And changing it will require more than small adjustments.

It will require disruption.

The End of the Slide

The slow slide does not continue indefinitely.

At some point, it reaches a threshold.

A point where the accumulation of small imbalances can no longer be ignored.

Where the effort becomes visible.

Where the cost becomes too high.

What This Chapter Is Saying

No one moment caused this.

No single decision created it.

It was built, slowly, through care, loyalty, patience, and the desire to make something work.

The Final Truth

You did more because you cared more.

You made excuses because you were loyal.

You told yourself every relationship has issues because you wanted this one to last.

And by the time you realize what it has become—

You are already deep inside it.

The Quiet Unraveling of Desire, Respect, and Connection

B y the time resentment becomes visible, it has already been forming for a long time.

It does not arrive as a sudden break, nor as a single moment of clarity.

It has emerged slowly, shaped by patterns that once felt reasonable—even loving.

What was once effort has become expectation. What was once chosen has become assumed.

And somewhere along the way, desire has begun to change.

What "When Desire Becomes Duty" Really Means
It is easy to misunderstand this phrase—to assume it refers only to sex.

But the shift runs deeper.

Desire becomes duty in the way she listens when she is already tired, soothes when she has nothing left to give, continues to be the reasonable one even when something in her wants to push back.

It appears in the moments where she initiates intimacy not from wanting—but from knowing it will prevent distance. In the way she smiles through disappointment, minimizes what she feels, and calls it compromise when, in truth, it is closer to self-abandonment.

None of this happens dramatically.

It happens quietly, through repetition, until it feels normal.

The Transformation of Love
Duty does not destroy love all at once.

If it did, the shift would be easier to recognize—and easier to resist.

Instead, it changes love gradually.

The first thing it alters is not the relationship itself, but the energy within it.

Erotic polarity softens. The sense of difference, tension, mutual desire begins to fade.

What remains is familiarity, stability, and a growing sense of effort.

From there, something else changes.

Admiration begins to thin. Not necessarily because either person has become worse, but because the dynamic between them has shifted. One gives more. One carries more. And that imbalance, even when unspoken, alters how each is seen.

Then softness goes. Not entirely—but enough to be noticed.

Patience becomes harder. Irritation appears more quickly. The emotional tone becomes heavier, less fluid, less generous.

Joy is the last to leave.

It does not disappear overnight. It recedes, gradually, replaced by a quieter, more muted experience.

Resentment as Signal

Resentment is often treated as a problem in itself, something to be managed, reduced, eliminated.

But resentment is not the origin.

It is the signal.

It is what surfaces when something has been unbalanced for too long, effort has not been matched, giving has not been reciprocated.

It is not irrational.

It is information.

The Years No One Names

For many women, this phase lasts longer than it should.

Years, sometimes.

Not because they are unaware, but because what they are experiencing is difficult to name.

There is no clear rupture. No single justification for leaving or demanding change. Just a growing sense that something is off, something has been lost, the relationship no longer feels the way it once did.

And yet—it continues.

What This Section Explores

This part of the book is about what relationships become when imbalance is left unexamined.

It examines the internal experience of carrying more than you should, for longer than you intended, and the quiet ways that experience reshapes how you feel, respond, and see the person beside you.

The Final Truth

Resentment is not the failure of love.

It is the evidence that something within it has been asked to carry too much.

And once it appears, it is asking to be understood.

Chapter 14

THE SILENT SCORECARD

You told yourself you weren't keeping score.

You believed that if love was real, it should not be measured. That generosity should be freely given, that care should not be conditional, that keeping a tally of who did what would reduce something meaningful to something transactional.

And so you did not keep score.

At least—not consciously.

The Body Keeps Track

But something in you was keeping track.

Not in numbers, not in a list you could point to or recite—but in a quieter, more persistent way. Your body registered what your mind chose not to hold.

It remembered how often you adjusted, let things go, gave more than you received. It held the weight of those moments, even when you dismissed them as insignificant.

You may not have been counting, but you were accumulating.

The Difference Between Counting and Feeling

Keeping score, in the way people warn against, suggests calculation. It suggests a deliberate tracking of inputs and outputs, a running ledger of fairness.

That is not what was happening.

What was happening was felt.

A gradual awareness, not always conscious, that something was not balanced. That effort was not evenly distributed. That care was flowing more in one direction.

You did not need to count it.

You could feel it.

Resentment as Unexpressed Anger

Resentment rarely presents itself as anger.

If it did, it might be easier to address. Anger has a clarity to it. It demands attention, insists on being heard, pushes toward confrontation or resolution.

Resentment is quieter. It simmers beneath the surface.

It is anger that has not been expressed, or has not been allowed to fully form. It is what remains when something has been felt but not said, noticed but not addressed, experienced but not validated.

It builds in the space where expression should have been.

Why It Goes Unexpressed

There are many reasons she does not express it.

Because it feels too small to justify. Because it might create conflict. Because she does not want to seem unreasonable or demanding. Because she tells herself it is not that serious.

And so she lets it pass.

Not once, but repeatedly.

The Accumulation of the Unsaid

Each unexpressed moment does not disappear.

It settles.

It becomes part of a growing internal record, not written down but deeply felt.

The time she let something go that mattered to her. The time she adjusted when she did not want to. The time she gave more than she had, and received less than she needed.

None of these moments, on their own, seemed large enough to confront.

Together, they form something else entirely.

The Shame of Wanting Reciprocity

At the centre of this is something more difficult than imbalance itself.

The shame of wanting it to be different.

The shame of wanting reciprocity.

Because wanting more can feel like asking too much. Like being needy, or demanding, or ungrateful for what is already there.

She tells herself she should not need this much. That she should be able to handle it, adjust, accept that no relationship is perfectly equal.

So she lowers her expectations.

Not dramatically, but incrementally.

The Internal Correction
When the feeling arises, she corrects herself.

He does a lot too.
I'm probably overthinking this.
It's not fair to expect everything to be equal.

These thoughts are not entirely wrong.

But they suppress the question rather than answer it.

The Moment Gratitude Changes
There is another shift that often goes unnoticed.

At the beginning, she feels grateful for what he does.

His effort is visible, meaningful, appreciated. What he offers feels like something given freely, something she receives with warmth.

Over time, something changes.

Not necessarily in what he does, but in how it is experienced.

What once felt like generosity becomes the baseline.

What once felt like effort begins to feel like the minimum.

And what she gives, increasingly, exceeds it.

From Gratitude to Expectation

This is not because she has become entitled.

It is because her own level of effort has risen.

When you are giving more, what you receive begins to feel smaller, even if it has not changed.

The gap between what is given and what is received becomes more noticeable.

And in that gap, something shifts.

The Quiet Withdrawal

She does not always express this directly.

Instead, she withdraws in smaller ways.

She becomes less enthusiastic, less open, less willing to give in the same way she once did. Not as a decision—but as a response.

Her energy changes.

Her tone shifts.

The ease that once defined the relationship becomes harder to access.

Why It Feels Confusing

From the outside, nothing dramatic has happened.

There has been no major conflict, no clear rupture, no single moment that explains the change.

And yet, she feels different.

More distant. More guarded. More easily irritated.

She may not immediately connect this to what has accumulated unspoken.

But that is where it lives.

The Weight of the Unacknowledged

What makes resentment particularly heavy is that it is rarely acknowledged, either by her or by him.

It exists in the space between what is happening and what is being said.

It is carried privately.

And because it is carried privately—it grows.

The Shift in Perception

Over time, the way she sees him begins to change.

Not dramatically, but subtly.

She notices what he does not do more than what he does. She becomes aware of the imbalance in ways that are difficult to ignore.

And once that awareness is established, it alters everything that follows.

Why It Is Hard to Reverse

By the time the scorecard becomes visible, it is already full.

Not in a literal sense, but in a felt one.

There is already a history, a pattern, a series of moments that have shaped how she experiences the relationship.

Addressing it now is no longer about one issue.

It is about many.

The Question Beneath the Feeling

Beneath resentment is a question that has not yet been asked out loud.

Why am I giving more than I am receiving?

And beneath that, an even more difficult one.

Why have I accepted this?

What This Chapter Is Asking You to See

Not that relationships must be perfectly balanced at all times.

But persistent imbalance, when unspoken, does not disappear.

It is stored. Felt. Carried.

The Final Truth
You did not keep score in the way you thought you might.

You did not track it, measure it, or hold it against him deliberately.

But your body remembered.

And over time, what it remembered became something you could no longer ignore.

Chapter 15

Sex as Obligation

(and Other Duties Required to Keep a Man)

I t does not feel like obligation at first.

If it did, it would be easier to refuse, name, resist—without confusion or self-doubt.

Instead, it arrives disguised as care, as attentiveness, as a quiet understanding of how relationships are maintained. It feels like maturity, like knowing what matters, like doing what is necessary to keep things good.

By the time it becomes obligation, it has already been something else for a long time.

The imbalance she feels does not stay internal. It begins to shape what she does.

The Subtle Humiliation of Maintenance Intimacy

There is a particular kind of humiliation that is difficult to describe, because it does not look like humiliation from the outside.

Nothing overt has happened. No one has demanded anything explicitly. There is no clear moment of coercion, no visible line crossed.

And yet—she knows.

She knows when she is participating in intimacy she does not fully want, for reasons she does not fully respect. When her body is present, but her desire is not. When she is doing something not out of wanting—but out of maintaining.

That is the humiliation.

Not that it is forced—but that it is chosen, repeatedly, for reasons that quietly diminish her.

From Insurance to Obligation

In the earlier stage, intimacy functioned as insurance, a way of keeping the relationship close, of preventing distance before it formed, of smoothing over moments that might otherwise create friction. It felt strategic, but still voluntary.

Now something has shifted.

The choice no longer feels entirely like a choice. It feels expected—not always by him, not always explicitly—but within the structure of the relationship she now inhabits.

She knows what happens if intimacy disappears. She has seen the withdrawal, the distance, the subtle shift in tone.

And so she does not wait for that to happen.

She pre-empts it.

The Fear Beneath It

Beneath this pattern is a fear rarely articulated—but deeply understood.

If I don't, he'll look elsewhere.

It is not always phrased so directly. Sometimes it appears in softer, more acceptable forms, ideas that sound like wisdom rather than pressure: "Physical connection is important." "Men feel love through intimacy."

But beneath these ideas sits something more primitive.

That sexual availability is tied to relational security.

That if she does not provide it, someone else will.

The Threat of Sexual Competition

This belief creates a quiet, constant sense of competition.

Not necessarily with a specific person—but with the possibility of one. With younger women, more available women, less complicated women, women who seem easier, more enthusiastic, more consistently responsive.

She may not consciously compare herself, but the standard exists.

And once it exists, it shapes behavior.

She becomes more accommodating, more responsive, more willing to override herself in order to remain preferable.

Trying Harder, Losing More

She tries to maintain the energy that once existed naturally.

She becomes more attentive, more available, more willing to meet what she perceives as the needs of the relationship. But effort cannot replicate desire.

And the more she tries to manufacture it, the more she feels the distance between what she is doing and what she wants.

This is where the humiliation deepens.

Because she is no longer just accommodating.

She is performing.

When Gratitude Disappears

At the beginning, her generosity may have been met with appreciation. There was a sense that what she gave was noticed, valued, received with warmth.

But over time, something changes.

What was once appreciated becomes expected.

What was once received with gratitude becomes part of the baseline.

And when gratitude disappears, the emotional exchange changes.

What she gives no longer feels like a gift.

It feels like something required to maintain the relationship.

Why Resentment Builds Here

This is where resentment takes on a sharper edge.

Because the imbalance is no longer subtle.

She is giving something deeply personal, something tied to her body, her desire, her sense of self. And she is giving it in a context where it no longer feels fully chosen.

There is no acknowledgment of the cost.

No recognition of what it requires for her to override herself.

And so the resentment is not only about frequency or desire.

It is about meaning.

Misaligned Desire

One of the most quietly destabilizing aspects of long-term relationships is not the absence of desire, but the mismatch of it.

Desire rarely declines in perfect synchrony. One partner wants more, or wants differently, or wants at different times. This, in itself, is not a failure. It is a normal part of human variation.

But what matters is how that mismatch is handled.

When desire is misaligned and unspoken, it becomes pressure. When it is acknowledged but not respected, it becomes resentment.

She begins to feel that her level of desire is a problem to be corrected. That her natural rhythm is insufficient, something that needs to be adjusted upward to meet an external standard.

The question shifts, subtly but significantly, from "What do I want?" to "What is enough?"

And "enough" is rarely defined by her.

The Pathologizing of Her Response
At this point, language begins to change.

What was once understood as variation becomes framed as deficiency.

Jokes appear first, light enough to dismiss.
"You're impossible to keep up with."
"You've gone cold lately."

Said with a smile, delivered in a tone that suggests playfulness, but carrying something sharper beneath.

If she reacts, she risks seeming humorless. If she ignores it, the message still lands.

Over time, the tone can shift.

What was once a joke becomes an accusation: Distant. Not interested. Frigid.

Words that reframe her experience as failure.

The Impact of Being Named This Way
There is a particular sting in being described this way.

Because it does not only comment on behavior, it assigns identity.

It suggests that something is wrong with her, that her desire is lacking, that she is the problem to be fixed.

And once that framing is introduced, it changes how she sees herself.

She becomes more self-conscious, more aware of her responses, more likely to override them.

Not because she wants to, but because she does not want to be *that* woman.

The Internalization

This is how obligation deepens.

Not through force—but through reframing.

If her lack of desire is a problem, then increasing her availability becomes a solution. If her natural rhythm is insufficient, then effort becomes necessary.

She begins to manage herself. To respond when she does not want to, initiate when she would not have, perform enthusiasm she does not feel.

Not because she is coerced, but because she has been positioned as responsible.

The Quiet Death of Erotic Energy

Erotic energy depends on freedom.

On the ability to want without pressure, to respond without calculation, engage without purpose beyond the experience itself.

Once intimacy becomes functional, once it serves as reassurance, maintenance, or correction, something essential is lost.

Desire cannot thrive under obligation.

It cannot be sustained through strategy.

And it cannot survive long in a space where it is quietly expected.

Free Desire vs Managed Intimacy

In the series *Fleabag*, desire is alive, unpredictable, often inconvenient.

It is not managed. Not used to stabilize anything. It appears suddenly, disrupts, pulls, complicates. And because of that, it feels real.

What stands in contrast is not simply the absence of desire elsewhere, but the presence of control.

Relationships where everything is stable, appropriate, well-maintained—and entirely devoid of that same energy.

It raises an uncomfortable question.

Whether desire survives more easily in spaces where nothing depends on it.

The Cultural Contract

What makes this dynamic particularly powerful is that it is not only personal.

It is cultural.

Women are socialized into a set of expectations that form an unspoken contract: **sex, agreeableness, labor, loyalty.**

- Sex as proof of love.

- Agreeableness as insurance.

- Emotional labor as rent.

- Self-erasure as loyalty.

These ideas are not presented as constraints.

They are framed as virtues. As what it means to be a good partner.

The Fear That Sustains It
At the centre of this contract is fear.

If I don't perform, I will be replaced.

This fear does not need to be stated to be effective. It is reinforced through stories, through advice, through the subtle ways women are taught to prioritize being chosen over being well.

And once it is internalized, it shapes behavior.

Not through force, but through anticipation.

The Invisible Checklist
Without ever writing it down, she begins to follow a checklist:
Be available.
Be responsive.
Be easy.
Do not create resistance.
Do not let things go cold.
Do not become someone he could leave.

She may not consciously agree to these rules.

But she lives by them.

When Partnership Becomes Performance

At this point, the relationship has shifted.

It is no longer a space of mutual desire.

It is a space of managed experience.

She is not only relating to him.

She is relating to the role she believes she must play to keep him.

And that role requires performance.

Emotional Labor as Maintenance

Sex is not the only thing being used to maintain the relationship.

It sits alongside emotional labor, alongside the work of keeping things smooth, of managing tone, preventing disruption.

Together, they form a system.

A system in which she is responsible for continuity.

The Breaking Point

At some point, something in her resists.

Not always dramatically, not always out loud, but unmistakably.

She no longer wants to override herself.

She no longer wants to participate in something disconnected from her own desire.

And the question becomes unavoidable:

Why am I doing this?

The Defiance
This is where the shift begins.

Not in behavior, but in perspective.

She begins to see the structure she has been operating within, to recognize the assumptions she has internalized, to question the idea that her role is to maintain, to reassure, to prevent.

A refusal.

Remind yourself:
- **Sex is not proof of love.**

Nor is it proof of loyalty or worth.

- **Sex is not a subscription fee for male companionship.**

It is not something owed in exchange for stability.

- **Sex is not a reward for male favors.**

You do not "owe" him access to your body. You do not owe him anything.

The Reclaiming of Desire

Desire, if it is to exist at all, must be free.

It must be chosen.

It must belong to her.

Anything else may sustain a relationship.

But it will not sustain her within it.

The Final Truth

Sex does not become obligation because desire disappears.

It becomes obligation because it is asked to do too much—to stabilize, reassure, secure, maintain, compensate for what is missing elsewhere.

And in being used for all of those things, it loses the one thing that made it meaningful.

It stops being *wanted*.

And once that happens, no amount of effort can bring it back.

Chapter 16

The Panic of Missing Out

There is a point in many long-term relationships where something begins to shift, not only in her, but in him.

It is not always obvious at first. It does not arrive as a conversation or a clearly stated concern.

It appears instead as a change in tone, frequency, expectation.

He begins to want more.

More intimacy. More responsiveness. More enthusiasm. More proof that what exists between them is still alive.

Her experience is not happening in isolation. It is being shaped in response to something else.

On the surface, this can look like desire.

Underneath, it is something else.

The Fear He Does Not Name

There is a fear many men do not articulate—and often do not fully recognize in themselves.

Time is passing.

Options narrow. Youth is no longer assumed. The sense of being able to start again, to find someone new, to access desire easily, begins to feel less certain.

This does not present as vulnerability. It presents as urgency.

He does not say, *I am afraid of what I am losing.*

He says, instead:
Why aren't we having more sex?
Why don't you want me like you used to?
Why has this changed?

The fear translates into demand.

The Escalation

At first, the increase is subtle.

He initiates more often. He notices rejection more quickly. He becomes more sensitive to fluctuations in her desire.

What might once have passed without comment now registers.

He pays attention. And then he responds.

The response is not withdrawal. It is pursuit.

When Desire Becomes Measurement

Intimacy begins to take on a new meaning for him.

It becomes a measure—of attraction, of validation, of whether the relationship is still intact.

Each interaction is no longer just an experience. It is information.

If she responds, things feel secure.

If she hesitates, something feels wrong. And so he seeks more of it.

Not because he is more desirous in a simple sense, but because he is trying to confirm something.

Her Experience of the Shift

From her perspective, the change feels different.

What he experiences as urgency, she experiences as pressure.

What he experiences as desire, she experiences as expectation.

The space that once allowed desire to emerge begins to narrow.

There is less room for spontaneity, less room for her own rhythm, less room for her to arrive at wanting in her own time.

Instead, there is anticipation. A sense that something is required.

The Feedback Loop

This is where the dynamic tightens.

The more he seeks reassurance through intimacy, the more she feels that intimacy is being asked to perform a function.

The more it is asked to perform, the less freely it arises.

The less freely it arises, the more he notices its absence.

And the more he notices its absence, the more he reaches for it.

The loop feeds itself.

Misreading the Withdrawal

He does not experience her response as pressure.

He experiences it as loss. Loss of attraction. Loss of interest. Loss of something that once felt secure.

And so he tries to correct it.

By initiating more, by pushing more directly, by questioning more openly.

But what he is responding to is not indifference. It is compression.

She is not withdrawing because she no longer cares.

She is withdrawing because the space for desire has been reduced.

The Demand for Enthusiasm

At this stage, it is not only frequency that matters.

It is quality.

He does not only want participation.

He wants enthusiasm. He wants to feel wanted.

This is where the pressure intensifies.

Because enthusiasm cannot be produced on demand.

It cannot be convincingly performed without cost.

And she feels that cost.

The Humiliation of Trying to Meet It

She may try, at least for a time. To be more responsive. More engaged. More present in the ways he seems to need.

But the more she tries, the more she becomes aware of the gap between what she is expressing and what she is feeling.

This is where the experience becomes quietly humiliating.

Not because she is being forced, but because she is attempting to produce something that is no longer naturally there.

And she knows it.

When Pressure Replaces Attraction

Attraction requires space. It requires the freedom to want, to move toward, to engage without expectation.

Pressure collapses that space.

When intimacy becomes something monitored, measured, and responded to, it ceases to be neutral.

It becomes loaded.

And what is loaded is difficult to desire.

The Gendered Asymmetry

This dynamic is rarely discussed clearly.

Men are often told that maintaining sexual connection is essential. That it is central to relationship health. That its absence signals a problem.

Women are often told, implicitly or explicitly, that responding to this need is part of maintaining the relationship.

The result is an asymmetry.

He seeks reassurance through intimacy. She provides intimacy to maintain stability.

But neither position allows desire to remain free.

The Escalation of Resentment

As this pattern continues, resentment deepens.

Not only because she feels pressured, but because the pressure is rarely acknowledged.

It is framed as need. As normal. As something she should understand.

And so her experience remains unnamed.

She is not seen as responding to pressure.

She is seen as someone withholding.

The Turning Point

At some point, something in her resists.

Not loudly at first—but clearly.

She becomes less willing to override herself.

Less willing to participate in something that feels increasingly disconnected from her own desire.

And the dynamic shifts again.

What This Chapter Is Saying

This is not a simple story of mismatched libido.

It is a pattern driven by fear on one side, adaptation on the other.

His fear of loss becomes demand. Her response to demand becomes withdrawal.

And the interaction between the two creates exactly what both are trying to avoid.

The Final Truth

The more intimacy is used to secure a relationship, the less it can sustain desire.

And when one person begins to pursue it out of fear—

And the other begins to provide it out of obligation—

What remains may look like connection—but it no longer feels like freedom.

Chapter 17

WHEN DESIRE BECAME DUTY

There is a scene in the film *The Hours*, based on the novel by Michael Cunningham, that lingers long after it ends.

It is a heart-wrenching scene many women recognize.

Laura Brown sits on the edge of her toilet, in the ensuite of her beautiful postwar American home.

Her life seems perfect—the kind of life she was meant to want.

Her husband is in bed, warm, expectant, calling gently in a sing-song voice, "Come to bed, Laura Brown."

Nothing about the moment is overtly wrong. There is no conflict, no cruelty, no visible fracture.

And yet—she cannot move.

She sits there, still, tears streaming down her face, not from panic, but from something quieter.

A kind of internal refusal she does not yet know how to name.

Because going to bed with him is not simply going to bed.

It is stepping into a role she can no longer inhabit.

It is responding in a way that no longer matches what she feels.

It is participating in something that, from the outside, looks like intimacy—but from the inside, feels like absence.

What makes the scene so unsettling is its *normality*.

There is no crisis to justify her distress. No story she could easily tell that would make sense to anyone else.

And that is precisely why so many women recognize it.

Because the moment when desire becomes duty does not announce itself.

It looks like this: A woman sitting quietly, unable to move toward something she is expected to want.

Not because she is dramatic. Not because she is ungrateful. But because she is quietly desperate.

Something inside her has already shifted—and she cannot pretend, not even for one more night, that it hasn't.

The End of Desire
There is no clear moment when desire ends.

No definitive point where she can say: *this is where it stopped.*

If anything, it lingers longer than it should. It flickers, returns in fragments, appears in moments that feel almost like before.

Enough to create doubt. Enough to make her question whether anything has truly changed.

But something has.

And what has replaced it is not the absence of intimacy, but a different kind of presence.

One that feels familiar on the surface—and entirely different underneath.

The Shift She Could Not Name

At first, it is not obvious.

She is still there. Still participating. Still responsive in the ways that matter externally. Nothing has collapsed. Nothing has been withdrawn in any visible sense.

But internally, something has shifted.

What was once spontaneous now feels anticipated. What was once mutual now feels directional. What was once driven by desire now feels shaped by expectation.

She does not immediately name this as duty.

She experiences it first as effort.

Mechanical Intimacy

The body continues.

This is what makes the shift so difficult to confront.

She knows the rhythm. She knows how to respond. She knows how to move through the experience in a way that appears natural, engaged, present.

And so she does.

But the experience has changed. It has become mechanical.

Not in the sense of being cold or entirely disconnected, but in the sense of being guided more by knowledge than by desire.

She knows what to do. She no longer feels why she is doing it.

The Gap Between Participation and Presence

This is where the internal split becomes more pronounced.

She is participating. But she is not fully present.

Part of her is engaged in the moment, responding, moving, maintaining.

Another part of her is observing, aware of the distance between what is happening externally and what she feels internally.

That gap is subtle at first.

But once it is noticed, it becomes difficult to ignore.

Emotional Dissociation

She does not experience this as a dramatic withdrawal. It is quieter than that.

A soft disengagement. A slight removal from the emotional centre of the experience. A sense of moving through something rather than being inside it.

She may still care about him. She may still want the relationship to work.

But in these moments, she is no longer fully there.

And she knows it.

Why She Continues

She continues for the same reasons she always has.

Because it maintains connection. Because it avoids tension. Because it feels easier than refusing, explaining, confronting what the refusal might reveal.

There is also habit.

The body remembers what the relationship has been. It continues along that path, even when the internal landscape has changed.

And so the pattern persists.

The Quiet Grief

What she feels is not only frustration or resentment.

It is grief.

Not loud, not dramatic, but persistent.

The grief of something that once felt alive now feeling managed. The grief of recognizing that desire cannot be summoned back through effort. The grief of realising that what has been lost is not just physical, but emotional.

And most difficult of all—

The grief of not wanting him in the way she once did.

The Thought She Avoids

There is a thought that begins to surface, one she does not immediately allow herself to articulate.

I don't want him.

Not always. Not in every moment. But enough that it matters.

Enough that it changes how she experiences the relationship.

She resists this thought.

She reframes it:
I'm just tired.
It's a phase.
It will come back.

Because accepting it feels final.

The Attempt to Restore

She may try to bring it back.

To reconnect, to create space for intimacy, to approach him differently, rediscover what once felt easy.

But desire does not respond to effort in that way.

It cannot be negotiated into existence.

And the more she tries to manufacture it, the more she becomes aware of its absence.

The Incompatibility

This is the point where something becomes clear, even if she does not yet fully accept it.

Desire and duty cannot coexist for long.

One eventually displaces the other.

And once duty has taken hold, desire struggles to return.

The Weight of Knowing

She begins to understand something she did not want to see.

That this is not just about a temporary mismatch, or a phase, or something that can be easily corrected.

It is about a deeper shift in how she relates to him.

And how she experiences herself in relation to him.

The Silence Around It

This stage is often lived in silence. Because it is difficult to explain without sounding harsh, unfair, or ungrateful.

There is no single complaint to point to.

Just a pervasive sense that something essential has changed.

The Beginning of the End

This is not necessarily where the relationship ends. But it is where something within it does.

The version of her that desired freely. The version of the relationship that felt mutual in that way.

It does not disappear all at once.

But it is no longer fully present.

What This Chapter Is Saying

This is not about failure.

Not hers, and not necessarily his.

It is about what happens when intimacy is asked to carry too much, for too long.

When it becomes responsible for maintaining connection, preventing distance, compensating for imbalance.

The Final Truth

Desire does not disappear suddenly.

It fades under pressure. Recedes under expectation.

And when it is replaced by duty, what remains may still look like intimacy—

But it no longer feels like desire.

Chapter 18

THE LOSS OF RESPECT

Every woman has a moment.

A look. A thought. Often quiet, difficult to name—when something changes in how she sees him.

It is not always dramatic. Not all at once. There is no single incident that explains it, no clear event she can point to and say: *this is when it happened.*

A realization: "I don't respect him anymore."

That is when the marriage truly shifts.

And once it has shifted, it does not return easily.

Respect Is Not Static

Respect is often assumed to be stable.

If it is present at the beginning, it will remain. If two people care about each other, it will sustain itself. It is treated as a given, something that exists alongside love without needing much attention.

But respect is not fixed.

It is shaped by behavior, by patterns, by the way two people meet each other over time.

And it is more fragile than most people realize.

The Conditions That Erode It

Respect does not disappear because of one failure.

It erodes through repetition.

Through small moments where something is not done, not said, not carried. Through patterns where one person consistently steps forward and the other does not.

It is shaped by what is required of each person in the relationship.

And in a dynamic where she is doing more, carrying more, managing more, something begins to change.

You Cannot Respect What You Compensate For

There is a particular difficulty in maintaining respect for someone you are consistently compensating for.

Not because they are unworthy of respect, but because the dynamic alters perception.

When she is the one who notices what needs to be done, initiates what needs to be addressed, carries what needs to be sustained – she begins to experience him differently.

Not as an equal participant.

But as someone she must account for.

This shift is subtle—but decisive.

Because respect depends, in part, on the sense that the other person can stand on their own within the relationship.

And when that sense weakens, respect follows.

The Hidden Cost of Over-Functioning

Her competence, her reliability, her willingness to step in, all qualities that once supported the relationship now begin to reshape it.

She becomes the stabilizing force.

He becomes, by comparison, less necessary.

Not because he lacks value, but because she has absorbed so much of the responsibility.

And in doing so, she has changed the structure.

She has made herself essential.

But she has also made him less so.

The Shift in How She Sees Him

This is not a conscious downgrade.

She does not decide to respect him less.

It happens gradually, through experience.

She notices what he does not do more than what he does. She becomes aware of the gaps, the things she has had to carry, the areas where she has stepped in repeatedly.

And once she sees it, she cannot unsee it.

The Loss of Admiration

Respect and admiration are closely linked.

Admiration requires a sense of strength, presence, someone who stands alongside you rather than behind you.

When she begins to feel that she is holding more than he is, that sense of admiration begins to thin.

Not because he has fundamentally changed, but because the dynamic between them has.

Why It Feels Unfair

This stage is often confusing.

Because she knows he is not entirely inadequate. He may be kind, intelligent, capable in other areas of life.

And yet, within the relationship, something feels off.

She feels more responsible. More aware. More engaged.

And that imbalance creates a tension that is difficult to resolve.

The Conflict Within Her

She does not want to lose respect for him.

She may try to correct herself, focus on his positive qualities, remind herself what drew her to him.

She may tell herself she is being too critical, too demanding, expecting too much.

But respect is not something restored through intention alone.

It responds to reality.

You Cannot Desire Someone You Manage

This is where the connection to desire becomes unavoidable.

Desire depends on difference, on a sense of the other person as separate, capable, self-directed.

But when she is managing him, even subtly, that sense changes.

She is no longer responding to him.

She is accounting for him.

And management is incompatible with desire.

You cannot desire someone you are responsible for in this way.

You cannot feel drawn toward someone you are, in some sense, holding up.

The Collapse of Polarity

Earlier, the loss of erotic energy may have been attributed to stress, to routine, to time.

Now it becomes clearer.

The dynamic itself has shifted.

The tension that once existed between them has flattened. The sense of mutuality has been replaced by asymmetry.

And without that tension, desire has nowhere to live.

Why It Rarely Returns

Once respect has been eroded in this way, it is difficult to restore.

Not impossible, but difficult.

Because it is not based on a single event that can be repaired. It is based on a pattern that has been repeated over time.

And patterns, once established, shape perception in lasting ways.

The Moment of Recognition

There is often a moment when she realizes it fully.

Not just that she is tired, not just that she is doing more—but that something deeper has changed.

She no longer looks at him in the same way.

She no longer feels the same pull, the same admiration, the same instinctive respect.

The recognition is sobering.

Because it is not a temporary state.

It is about a structural shift.

Why She Stayed Past This Point

Many women remain in the relationship even after this shift has occurred.

Because leaving is not simple. Because there are shared lives, shared histories, shared responsibilities.

Because part of her still hopes that something can be restored.

That if the dynamic changes, the feeling will return.

Sometimes it does.

Often, it does not.

What This Chapter Is Saying

The loss of respect is not a moral failing.

It is not something she has chosen.

It is the natural consequence of a dynamic in which one person carries more than they should—for longer than they should.

The Final Truth

Love can survive many things.

But it struggles to survive the loss of respect.

And once respect has eroded, quietly and consistently, over time—

It takes more than effort to bring it back.

It takes a complete restructuring of the relationship.

And sometimes, by the time that is understood—it is already too late.

Chapter 19

THE LONELINESS INSIDE MARRIAGE

Loneliness is not always the absence of another person.

Sometimes—it is their presence.

After the shift in how she sees him, something else begins to emerge.

Being Unseen in Plain Sight

There is a particular kind of loneliness that exists within relationships, one that is difficult to explain to anyone who has not experienced it.

From the outside, nothing appears wrong.

She is partnered. She is not alone. There is someone beside her, someone who shares her life, her space, her routines.

And yet—she feels unseen.

Not in a dramatic sense. Not as though she has been entirely ignored or rejected. But in a quieter, more persistent way.

The deeper parts of her experience do not land.

Her internal world—her thoughts, her fatigue, her shifting emotional land-scape—moves past him without recognition.

She can speak and not feel heard. Explain and not feel understood. Be physically present—and still feel invisible.

The Subtle Disconnection

This is not always the result of neglect. Often, it is the result of misalignment.

She has changed. The relationship has changed. The dynamic between them has shifted in ways that are difficult to articulate.

And yet, the structure remains.

They continue to move through the routines of partnership, sharing space, responsibilities, a life that, on the surface, still functions.

But something essential is missing.

The Exhaustion of Explaining Yourself

At first, she tries to bridge the gap.

She explains what she is feeling. She puts words to things that are not easy to articulate. She tries to bring him into her experience.

She chooses her language carefully, trying to be clear without being harsh, honest without overwhelming.

But something does not translate.

She finds herself repeating. Rephrasing. Softening. Trying again.

Each attempt requires effort. And each time the response falls short, it feels heavier.

When Language Stops Working

Over time, she begins to realize that the issue is not simply one of wording. It is not that she has failed to explain it well enough.

It is that what she is trying to communicate cannot be easily received within the existing dynamic.

So she explains less. Not as a decision—but as a response.

She begins to keep more to herself, not because it does not matter, but because expressing it no longer feels effective.

The Internal Withdrawal

This is where the loneliness deepens.

Not in the absence of conversation—but in the absence of being met.

She becomes quieter, not in volume, but in depth. She shares less of what is actually happening for her. Less nuance. Less complexity.

She remains present in the relationship. But not fully.

The Weight of Carrying It Alone

The things she once processed with him, she now carries by herself. Her thoughts. Her questions. Her frustrations. Her realizations. Her quiet desperation.

There is no longer a sense of shared understanding, of mutual reflection.

There is only her.

This is what makes the loneliness so acute.

Not that she is alone in life.

But that she is alone in her experience of it.

The Moment It Becomes Clear
There is often a moment, or a series of moments, where this becomes undeniable.

A conversation that goes nowhere. An attempt to connect that falls flat. A realization she has stopped expecting to be understood.

It is not always dramatic.

But it is decisive.

Why It Feels So Heavy
Because partnership is meant to mitigate loneliness.

It is meant to provide a sense of being known, of being seen, of being accompanied in the deeper parts of life.

When that is missing, the contrast is stark.

She is not just alone. She is alone while being partnered.

The Comparison She Avoided

At some point, she begins to consider something she once resisted.

What would it feel like to be alone?

Not in the abstract—but in reality.

And the answer is not what she expected.

Why Being Alone Feels Lighter

Because being alone removes the dissonance.

There is no expectation of being understood that goes unmet. No repeated effort to explain something that does not land. No sense of being unseen in the presence of someone who is meant to see you.

Alone, she is simply alone. And there is clarity in that.

The loneliness of partnership is different.

It is layered with expectation, effort, the quiet disappointment of something that should exist but does not.

The Realization She Could Not Avoid

This is the point where something shifts internally.

She begins to understand the relationship is no longer protecting her from loneliness.

It is, in some ways, creating it.

And this realization is difficult to hold. Because it challenges the fundamental assumption that partnership is better than being alone.

What This Chapter Is Saying

Loneliness inside a relationship is not a failure of gratitude.

It is not a sign that she is asking for too much.

It is the natural response to not being met, over time, in ways that matter.

The Final Truth

It is possible to be surrounded and still feel alone.

It is possible to be partnered and still feel unseen.

And sometimes, the most honest thought she has is this: *I felt less alone when I was by myself.*

And for the first time, she begins to understand the cost of staying.

The question is no longer what is happening—but what she will do about it.

PART IV: THE BREAKING POINT

Conflict, Suspension, and the End of the Old Pattern

There is a moment in a relationship when what has been contained begins to show.

It appears in something small. A comment. A tone. A reaction that feels disproportionate to what is happening in the moment.

But what is surfacing is not the moment itself. It is everything that has been building beneath it.

Because resentment can be carried for a long time.

Longer than most expect—longer than seems reasonable from the outside.

It settles into the structure of the relationship, shaping tone, behavior, what is said and what is left unsaid.

For a while, it coexists with everything else. With routine. With shared history. With the practicalities of a life built together.

It does not disrupt immediately.

But resentment is not passive. It does not remain contained.

It accumulates pressure, quietly at first—then with increasing insistence.

And eventually, something gives.

The End of Containment

The shift into this phase is not always dramatic—but it is unmistakable.

What was once managed can no longer be managed. What was once tolerated becomes harder to absorb.

The effort required to keep everything steady begins to exceed what she is willing—or able—to give.

She becomes less patient. Less accommodating. Less willing to smooth over what has been smoothed too many times.

This is when conflict becomes more visible.

Not because conflict has suddenly appeared, but because it is no longer absorbed.

What It Looks Like From the Outside

From the outside, it can look like she has changed. She seems sharper. Less forgiving. More reactive. Less willing to let things go.

It may appear something has gone wrong.

But what has happened is something else.

She has stopped compensating.

The Release of What Was Held

What emerges in this phase is not new.

It is what has been there all along—held back, managed, contained.

The frustrations that were minimized. The needs that were deferred. The moments that were let go.

They begin to surface. Not always cleanly or proportionately.

Because they are not coming from one moment. They are coming from many.

The Misinterpretation

This stage is often misunderstood.

It is interpreted as escalation, deterioration, the relationship becoming worse.

But in many ways, it is the first moment of honesty. Not necessarily calm, not necessarily constructive, but honest.

The woman who once managed everything is no longer doing so.

And what remains is what has always been underneath.

The Turning Point

This is where the relationship reaches a threshold.

It can no longer continue in the same form without something changing.

Either the dynamic shifts, in a meaningful, sustained way—

Or the relationship itself begins to unravel.

What This Section Explores

This part is not about subtle shifts.

It is about what happens when those shifts can no longer be contained.

When resentment becomes visible. When it finds expression. When it moves from internal experience to external reality.

It is about conflict that is not really about what it appears to be.

About separation that feels both devastating and relieving.

About anger that arrives late, but with force.

The Final Truth

Resentment is not the end of the story.

It is the point at which the story can no longer continue as it has.

What follows is not always graceful.

But it is often the first time something real begins.

Chapter 20

The Fight Wasn't About the Dishes

I t rarely begins with what it appears to be.

A comment about the kitchen. A tone that lands the wrong way. A small moment—ordinary enough that it would not have mattered before.

And yet—this time, it does.

Conflict as Symptom
From the outside, it looks disproportionate.

The reaction is too strong. The response too sharp. The escalation too quick for something so minor.

Why does this matter so much?

But the question is misplaced.

Because the conflict is not about the moment.

It is about what the moment represents.

The unwashed dishes are not the issue.

They are the visible edge of something that has been building quietly for a long time.

What the Argument Is Really About

It is about imbalance.

About who notices and who does not. Who carries and who assumes. Who adjusts and who remains unchanged.

It is about the accumulation of small moments where she did more, said less, absorbed what could have been shared.

The dishes are simply the point at which that accumulation becomes impossible to ignore.

The Breaking of Restraint

For a long time, she has contained it.

She has chosen when to speak, when to let things go.

She has softened her tone, minimized her reactions, prioritized stability over expression.

She has managed.

And because she has managed, the relationship has appeared functional.

But management has a limit.

At some point, the effort required to contain everything exceeds the effort required to release it.

When that threshold is crossed, restraint gives way.

The Explosion

What follows can feel sudden.

A sharpness that was not there before. Words that are more direct—less filtered, less careful. Frustration that no longer disguises itself as patience.

To him, it may feel like an overreaction.

To her, it feels like a release.

Because what is being expressed is not just about this moment.

It is about all the moments that came before it.

Why, To Him, It Feels Out of Proportion

He experiences the argument in isolation. She experiences it in context.

He sees one incident. She feels a pattern.

And because he does not feel the pattern, the intensity of her response seems unjustified.

The Language of the Argument

Often, the words do not match the depth of what is being expressed.

The argument may stay at the level of the immediate issue.

You never help.

Why should I have to ask?

Why am I the only one who notices?

But underneath these statements is something more fundamental:

Why am I carrying this alone?

The First Honest Conflict

This may be the first time she is no longer filtering herself to preserve the relationship.

The first time she allows the full weight of her frustration to surface without correcting or softening it.

It is not necessarily constructive.

But it is real.

His Experience of the Shift

From his perspective, something has changed.

She is different. More reactive. More critical. Less patient.

He may say it directly. "You've changed."

And in one sense, he is right.

What He Means

What he often means is this:

You are no longer behaving in the way I am used to.

Translation: You are no longer absorbing what you once absorbed.

The version of her that maintained the relationship has shifted.

And he is responding to that shift.

What She Hears
What she hears is something else.

That the problem is her reaction, rather than the pattern that produced it.

That the issue is her change, rather than the dynamic that made the change necessary.

And this deepens the conflict.

The Collapse of the Old Dynamic
The argument marks a turning point.

Not because of what was said, but because of what is no longer being done.

She is no longer containing everything. She is no longer compensating in the same way. She is no longer maintaining the previous equilibrium.

And without that maintenance, the underlying imbalance becomes visible.

Why It Feels Like Things Are Getting Worse
To him, it may feel like the relationship is deteriorating.

There is more conflict. More tension. More friction than before.

But what has changed is not the presence of conflict.

It is the absence of suppression. What was once held inside is now being expressed.

The Irreversibility

Once this stage is reached, it is difficult to return to what existed before.

Not because the relationship cannot change, but because she cannot unsee what she now sees.

She cannot return to the version of herself that absorbed everything quietly.

That version required not knowing, or not fully acknowledging, what was happening.

And now she does.

What This Chapter Is Saying

The fight is not about the dishes.

It is about the distribution of responsibility, of attention, of care.

It is about the invisible structure of the relationship becoming visible, often for the first time.

The Final Truth

Arguments like this are not the beginning of the problem.

They are the end of its concealment.

And when something that has been hidden for a long time is finally expressed—

It rarely comes out quietly.

Chapter 21

THE IN-BETWEEN

Resentment does not always end a relationship. More often, it changes how the relationship is experienced from within.

At first, resentment is something she carries. It sits alongside everything else—routine, moments of connection, the practical life they have built together.

Over time, it becomes something else.

It stops being a feeling that comes and goes, becoming a lens through which the relationship is seen.

What once felt neutral now feels weighted. What once felt manageable now feels effortful. What once felt like compromise now feels like loss.

This is where the shift begins.

Not in what is happening externally—but in how she feels about staying.

She begins to notice that the relationship no longer restores her. That being inside it requires more than it gives back. That the version of herself she has to be in order to remain is no longer one she can sustain.

The Half-Detached Life

This is where the in-between begins.

She is still there—but not in the same way.

She participates—with distance. She engages—without the same investment. She moves through the routines of the relationship, but something essential has been withdrawn.

From the outside, very little appears different.

From the inside, everything does.

Knowing, But Not Leaving

She knows.

Not always in a single, decisive moment, but in a series of recognitions that accumulate into certainty.

Something is over.

Not the logistics of the relationship—not yet.

The routines continue. The conversations continue. The shared life remains in place.

But internally, something has shifted in a way that does not reverse.

And still—she stays.

Why She Doesn't Leave Immediately
Leaving is not a thought.

It is a process.

There are practical considerations. Shared homes, shared finances, shared responsibilities. The architecture of a life that cannot be dismantled in a single decision.

There are emotional considerations. History, attachment, the memory of what the relationship once was, and the hope, however faint, that something might still be recoverable.

And then there is something quieter.

The difficulty of acting on what she now knows.

The End of Arguing
One of the first things to disappear is the intensity of conflict.

Not because things have improved. But because she is no longer trying in the same way.

The arguments that once carried urgency now feel unnecessary.

She does not push as hard. She does not insist in the same way. She lets more pass, not out of patience, but out of disengagement.

This can look like calm.

It is not calm—it is detachment.

The Quiet Reorganization

At the same time, something else begins.

She starts to reorganize her life internally.

She imagines what it would look like to live differently. She considers practicalities she once avoided. She begins to separate, not physically, but psychologically.

This is not always conscious. But it is deliberate in its own way.

Still Performing, But Less Convincingly

There is still a degree of performance. She shows up. She participates. She maintains enough of the structure that the relationship continues to function.

But it is thinner now. Less convincing. More effortful.

And she feels that effort.

The Loneliness Shifts Shape

The loneliness that once came from being unseen now takes on a different form.

It becomes the loneliness of knowing something the other person does not.

She sees the end.

He may not.

And so she moves through the relationship carrying a truth that is not yet shared.

The Last Attempts

Sometimes, there are attempts to repair.

Conversations that are more direct. Efforts to reset, to reconnect, to see if something can still be restored.

But these attempts feel different. Less hopeful. More evaluative.

She is no longer trying to make it work at any cost.

She is trying to see if it can work at all.

When It Becomes Clear

At some point, the ambiguity fades. Not suddenly, but definitively.

She realizes she is not waiting for change. She is waiting for the moment she is ready to act.

And that moment does not arrive all at once.

It builds.

The Emotional Disconnection

By the time she leaves, much of the emotional separation has already occurred.

The grief has begun, quietly, while she was still inside the relationship. The detachment has already taken place, layer by layer.

This is why the leaving can appear sudden.

Because the internal process is not visible from the outside.

Why Others Don't See It

To others, it may seem abrupt. Unexpected.

But they have not seen the in-between.

They have not seen the building resentment, the gradual withdrawal, the quiet recognition, the slow reorganisation of a life that is no longer aligned.

The Threshold

Eventually, something shifts.

The cost of staying becomes greater than the cost of leaving.

This is the threshold.

It is not dramatic. But it is decisive.

What This Chapter Is Saying

There is a phase between knowing and leaving.

A space where the relationship continues externally, but has already changed internally.

It is quiet. Often invisible.

But it is where the real transition happens.

The Final Truth

By the time she leaves, she has already been gone for some time.

The departure is not the beginning of the ending.

It is the moment it becomes visible.

Chapter 22

Divorce as Detox?

I t is easy to believe leaving is what fixes things.

That once the relationship ends, the weight lifts because he is gone.

But what changes most profoundly is not always who is beside her. It is *how she was living within the relationship.*

The constant adjustment. The quiet over-functioning. The effort to hold everything together.

When that pattern is removed, something shifts immediately.

Whether she leaves or stays—it is not the ending that changes everything.

It is *the refusal to continue in the same way.*

If Ongoing Resentment Means the Relationship Is Unsalvageable

Separation or divorce may be extreme. But they may become unavoidable if resentment remains.

Unless she makes an adjustment, unless she refuses to continue in the same pattern, ending the relationship may be preferable.

But what she then has to avoid is bringing the same patterns into future relationships.

The Extreme of Leaving

The moment after a relationship changes, or ends, is not always what people expect.

There is an assumption that grief will arrive immediately, that the dominant feeling will be loss, that the absence of the relationship will be felt as a sudden and overwhelming void.

Sometimes it is.

But often, something else comes first.

The Unexpected Relief

There is a lightness that appears before anything else has time to settle.

Not joy, not happiness, not even clarity.

Relief.

The constant monitoring stops. The need to anticipate, adjust, manage, hold everything together—falls away almost overnight.

She is no longer responsible for the emotional temperature of the relationship. No longer scanning for shifts in tone, no longer calculating when to speak and when to let things pass.

The background noise disappears.

And in its absence, something in her body exhales.

The Nervous System Reset

What lifts first is not love.

It is strain.

The strain of over-functioning. The strain of carrying more than she should have—for longer than she should have. The strain of maintaining something that required constant attention to remain intact.

When that strain is removed, the body responds before the mind has time to interpret what has happened.

There is space. There is quiet. There is a kind of stillness that had not been available for a long time.

What Actually Changed

It is easy, at this point, to assume that what brought relief was the absence of him.

But that is not always true.

What has been removed is not only the person.

It is the role she was inhabiting.

The one who noticed first. The one who adjusted. The one who carried what was not shared.

That role can disappear inside a relationship, just as it can disappear when one ends.

And when it does, the effect is the same.

Detox, Not Escape

What she is experiencing is not simply freedom.

It is detox.

The removal of something that had been saturating her experience for a long time. Something she had adapted to so gradually that she no longer recognized its weight.

When that weight is lifted, the system does not immediately collapse into grief.

It recalibrates.

The Absence of Constant Demand

For the first time in a long time, there is no one requiring anything from her in that specific way.

No expectation to manage, to respond, to maintain.

No need to interpret another person's moods, or to adjust herself in response to them.

She can move through her day without that layer of awareness.

And that absence is profound.

The Return of Self

Something else begins to reappear.

Not dramatically—but gradually: A sense of herself that had been pushed to the side.

Her preferences. Her rhythms. Her way of moving through the world without constant consideration of how it will be received.

She begins to notice what she wants again.

Not what will work. Not what will keep things smooth.

What she actually wants.

Why It Comes Before Grief

Grief requires space.

And space is what has just been restored.

When she was inside the pattern, much of that space was occupied.

By effort. By attention. By the ongoing work of maintaining something that required constant engagement.

There was little room left for reflection. Little room left for feeling.

Now, that space exists.

But it does not fill immediately.

The Quiet Before the Drop

There is often a period where things feel unexpectedly manageable.

She is functioning. Sleeping. Moving through her life with a sense of ease that had been missing.

It may even feel, at times, like she has already moved on.

But this is not the end of the process.

It is the beginning of it.

When Grief Arrives

Grief comes later.

Not all at once, and not always in a way that is immediately recognisable.

It arrives in moments.

A memory that surfaces without warning. A recognition of what was hoped for, but never fully realized. A sense of loss that is not only about the person, but about the version of the future that will not exist.

This is when the emotional reality begins to settle.

The Difference Between Ending and Changing

For some women, this process follows the end of a relationship.

For others, it begins while they are still inside it.

Because what is being removed is not always the relationship itself.

It is the way they were relating within it.

The over-functioning. The accommodation. The quiet, constant management.

And when that stops, something shifts.

Whether she stays or leaves—the system no longer holds.

What This Chapter Is Saying

This chapter is not saying "leaving will fix it".

It is saying that removing the pattern changes everything—whether or not the relationship ends.

If it ends, relief is not proof that the relationship did not matter.

It is evidence of what was being carried within it.

And what lifts first is not always love.

It is the burden.

The Final Truth

Exhaustion lifts before grief arrives.

Not because he is gone.

But because she is no longer living the way she was when she was with him.

And that change is where everything begins.

Chapter 23

THE RAGE STAGE

There is a phase many women do not expect.

Not because they do not feel anger, but because of the scale of it.

It arrives. After the leaving. After the relief. After the initial quiet—after the first sense that something heavy has been put down.

And then—suddenly or gradually—it surfaces.

Rage.

Necessary, Not Excessive
This anger can feel disproportionate.

Too intense. Too late. Too consuming for what is, externally, already over.

She may question it:
Why now?
Why this much?
Why does it feel like this?

But this is not new anger.

It is stored anger.

It is everything that was not said during the quiet resentment stage, when it first needed to be said.

Everything that was minimized, softened, explained away, or absorbed—in the name of keeping things stable.

It is not excessive. It is accumulated.

Anger at Him

Some of the anger is directed outward. At what he did not see. What he did not carry. What he did not change—even when it became clear something needed to. At the ways he benefited from the imbalance.

Not necessarily intentionally, not always consciously, but consistently.

At the expectations that were placed on her, sometimes explicitly, often implicitly, and rarely questioned.

She sees it more clearly now.

Without the need to maintain the relationship, without the pressure to interpret generously or minimize impact, the dynamic appears sharper.

And the anger follows.

Anger at Herself

But the anger does not stop there.

Some of it turns inward. At the ways she adapted. The ways she overrode herself—stayed longer than she should have, accepted what did not feel right, explained what did not need to be explained. At the moments she knew, but did not act. At the times she silenced herself, softened her reactions, chose stability over truth.

This anger can feel more difficult to hold.

Because it is directed at someone she understands intimately.

Herself.

Anger at the Years

There is also grief that appears as anger.

At time itself. At the years spent trying to make something work that was not working in the way she needed it to. At the energy invested, the effort given, the parts of herself that were shaped around maintaining something that could not be sustained in that form.

It is not only about what happened.

It is about how long it happened for.

Why It Comes After

This stage does not arrive earlier because it could not.

While she was inside the relationship, anger had to be managed. Contained. Softened. Redirected. Made smaller so that the relationship could continue.

There was no space for it to exist fully.

Now there is.

The Fear of Becoming Bitter

This is where many women become concerned.

They worry that this anger will define them. That it will harden into bitterness, into something that lingers too long and reshapes how they see everything that comes after.

They may feel pressure to move through it quickly. To forgive. To let go. To rise above it.

But premature resolution does not dissolve anger.

It suppresses it again.

Rage as Information

Anger, in this context, is not the problem. It is information.

It points to where boundaries were crossed. Where needs were not met. Where imbalance was sustained for too long.

It reveals what mattered. What hurt. What should not have been carried alone.

Seen this way, anger is not destructive.

It is clarifying.

The Function of Rage

Rage, at its most intense, has a purpose.

It separates. It creates distance from what was tolerated. It breaks the instinct to minimize, to reinterpret, to soften what happened. It allows her to see the relationship, and her role within it, without distortion.

This clarity can feel sharp.

But it is clean.

Moving Through, Not Past

The goal is not to eliminate this anger as quickly as possible.

It is to move through it. To allow it to surface, to understand what it is pointing to, to let it complete its function.

When it is avoided, it lingers.

When it is acknowledged, it moves.

The Shift Within It

Over time, the intensity changes.

Not because the truth of it disappears, but because it has been fully felt.

The sharp edges soften. The urgency fades. The need to revisit it diminishes.

What remains is not rage. It is understanding.

What This Chapter Is Saying

Anger, in this stage, is not a failure.

She is not bitter. She is responding.

It is a response to what has been experienced, often over a long period of time, without full expression.

A response to the resentment years.

It is part of the process of reclaiming clarity, boundaries, and self-trust.

And once that response has been fully allowed—it no longer needs to carry the same force.

The Final Truth

Beneath the anger, beneath the clarity it brings, something steadier starts to take shape.

She is no longer reacting in the same way. No longer trying to be understood, or to make something work that no longer holds.

The urgency fades. The need to explain fades with it.

What remains is not the relationship, and not the anger.

It is her.

And for the first time in a long time, she is no longer orienting herself around what is in front of her—but around what she can now see clearly.

PART V: After the Pattern

How She Stops Performing, Wherever She Lands

By the time she reaches this point, the question is no longer whether the relationship survived.

It is whether she can return to being the woman who made it possible.

Because what has broken is not only the structure of the relationship.

It is the pattern that sustained it.

And once that pattern is seen, once it is felt in the body—understood in its full weight—it cannot be quietly resumed.

Whatever happens next, whether she leaves or stays, whether the relationship ends or reshapes itself, one thing is no longer available to her.

She cannot disappear in the same way again.

That is where something new begins.

What Changes Now

This is not the part where everything becomes easy.

It is the part where everything becomes *clear.*

By this stage, she understands something she did not before.

Resentment was not an accident. It was the result of a pattern.

A pattern of over-functioning. Anticipating. Adjusting. Giving more than was returned—and calling it love.

A pattern of staying past the point of ease. Smoothing past the point of truth. Maintaining something that required her to disappear in order to continue.

And once she sees that pattern, she cannot unsee it.

This Is Not About Being Alone

This part of the book is not about what happens when she is single.

It is not about independence as an identity, or solitude as a solution.

Because the pattern does not depend on a relationship.

It depends on her.

She can carry it into anything.

Into a new relationship. Into a better relationship. Into a relationship with someone who, on the surface, is entirely different.

If the pattern remains, the outcome eventually does too.

The End of Performance

What changes now is not her desire for connection.

It is how she relates to it.

No longer trying to secure a relationship. No longer trying to be the version of herself that will make it work. No longer anticipating what is needed and becoming it before it is asked.

She stops performing.

Not dramatically. Not as a rejection of care or generosity.

But as a refusal to organize herself around being chosen.

What She No Longer Does

She no longer manages what is not hers.

She no longer fills in gaps before they are acknowledged.

She no longer uses her body to stabilize something that is unstable.

She no longer explains herself repeatedly in the hope of being understood.

She no longer waits to see if something that feels wrong will correct itself over time.

And most importantly—*she is no longer afraid of losing the relationship.*

The Real Shift

This is the shift everything else depends on.

As long as she is afraid of losing him, she will adapt. She will soften, adjust, compensate—perform in ways that feel small in the moment but accumulate over time.

When that fear lifts, something else becomes possible.

She no longer needs to manage what happens next. She no longer needs to secure the outcome.

She can see the relationship clearly—and respond from that clarity, rather than from fear.

Not a New Set of Rules

This is not a checklist. Not a new way to get it right.

It is the absence of a strategy.

She is no longer trying to manage the relationship into stability.

She allows it to show what it is—and then decides whether it is something she wants to be inside.

The Difference Now

Before, she asked: *How do I make this work?*

Now, she asks: *Does this work for me?*

It is a quieter question. But it changes everything.

The Final Truth

She did not become harder to love.

She became unwilling to disappear in order to be loved.

And wherever she goes next, that is what she carries with her.

Chapter 24

No Longer Trying to Be Chosen

She does not arrive here all at once.

There is no single decision that marks the shift. No clear moment where everything changes.

It happens more quietly than that.

After the anger has moved through her, after the urgency has settled, something else begins to take its place.

Not effort. Not strategy.

Attention.

She is no longer trying to be chosen in the same way.

She is watching—not for signs of interest, reassurance, or potential, but for something simpler.

What is actually there.

This is the first real change—not what she does, but what she *no longer does.*

She does not lean in to stabilize what feels uncertain. She does not offer more to see if it will be returned. She does not adjust herself to maintain interest.

She lets what is there reveal itself—without interference.

She notices it almost immediately.

The absence of the old instinct.

The urge to adjust, anticipate, shape herself into what might be wanted before it is asked. The quiet calculation of how to be easier, more agreeable, more likely to be chosen.

It is not there in the same way anymore.

Not because she has decided to resist it. But because something in her no longer agrees to it.

She has seen what that version of herself required. What it cost. What it slowly turned love into.

And once that is understood—not intellectually but viscerally—it is difficult to return to it without feeling the strain immediately.

So she does something different.

Not dramatically. But decisively.

She does not try to be chosen.

The End of the Subtle Performance

Before, it was almost invisible.

The way she would listen for cues, adjust her tone, soften her opinions, anticipate what might create ease. The way she would offer more of herself early, not because she was asked, but because it felt like the right thing to do.

It did not feel like performance. It felt like connection.

But it had a direction.

It moved her slightly away from herself—toward being selected.

How Early It Begins

This pattern rarely begins during long-term relationships.

It begins at the start.

In the early stages, when everything feels open, when attraction is forming, when the stakes are quietly present.

She pays attention.

Not only to him, but to how she is being received.

Does he like this? Is this too much? Should I say less?

These adjustments are small.

But they accumulate.

And over time, they form a version of her that is easier to choose—and harder to sustain.

Why It Worked

Because it was rewarded.

She was seen as easy, warm, low-maintenance.

She created comfort. She reduced friction.

And that often led to what she wanted.

He stayed.

But what was reinforced was not her.

It was the version of her that made staying easy.

The Realization

This is what she sees now.

That being chosen is not the same as being known.

That being kept is not the same as being met.

That a relationship built on adaptation will require ongoing adaptation to sustain.

And she is no longer willing to do that.

What She Does Instead

She does not adjust in advance. She speaks as she is. She allows moments to be slightly uncomfortable. She lets her responses be real—not optimized.

She does less.

Not to test him. Not to create distance.

But because she is no longer organizing herself around being chosen.

The Shift in Direction

Before, she was oriented toward securing the relationship.

Now, she is oriented toward understanding it.

She is no longer asking: How do I make this work?

She is asking: Does this work for me?

And she does not rush the answer.

The Quiet Confidence

This does not look like confidence in the way it is often described.

It is not loud. Not declarative.

It is the absence of urgency.

The absence of needing to make something happen quickly. The absence of needing to secure interest before it fades.

She can let things unfold. Because she is no longer trying to control the outcome.

What This Chapter Is Saying

Being chosen is not the goal.

Not if it requires her to become someone else in order to achieve it.

Because anything built that way will require her to remain that way.

And she already knows where that leads.

The Final Truth

She does not try to be chosen.

She allows herself to be seen.

And then she decides—whether the person in front of her is someone she actually wants to stay with.

The power sits with *her evaluation, not his selection.*

Chapter 25

REFUSING TO MANAGE WHAT IS NOT HERS

There was a time when she believed this was part of love.

The ability to sense what was unspoken. To notice shifts in tone, mood, energy. To step in early—to soften, to stabilize.

She did not think of it as management. She thought of it as care.

The Habit of Stepping In

She still sees everything.

The pause in his voice. The shift in his mood. The moment something tightens in the space between them.

She knows exactly what it means.

And exactly what she could do. A question to ask. A tone to soften. A way to move things back into ease.

The skill is still there.

What She No Longer Does

But this is where it changes.

She does not step in.

The instinct rises, as it always did—and she lets it pass.

Not because she does not care.

But because she recognizes what belongs to her—and what does not.

The Pause

He is quiet.

She notices.

There is a space where she would once have filled the silence, redirected the moment, restored connection before it slipped.

She feels that pull. And she stays still.

The Discomfort

This is not easy.

The moment stretches. The ease does not return immediately.

She feels the tension in her body—the urge to fix it.

And she does *nothing.*

This is Not Indifference

This is not withdrawal.

She is not becoming cold. Not withholding.

She is present.

She is aware.

But she is no longer taking responsibility for what is not hers to carry.

The End of Mood Management

His mood is his.

His internal state is his.

She does not adjust herself to compensate for it.

She does not reorganize the moment to make it easier.

She allows him to have his experience—without stepping in and regulating it for him.

The End of Translation

She no longer explains him to himself.

She does not interpret what he feels before he names it.

She does not soften his meaning or reframe his words.

If something needs to be said—he can say it.

What This Requires

Restraint.

Not action. Not effort. Restraint.

The ability to see exactly what she could do—and not do it.

The Internal Shift

Before, she moved toward the discomfort.

She absorbed it, worked with it, reshaped it.

Now, she allows it to exist.

Without immediately changing it.

Without making it her responsibility.

What This Chapter Is Saying

Care is not the same as management.

Connection is not created by one person stabilising everything.

And when she stops carrying what is not hers—she is no longer exhausted by the relationship.

The Final Truth

She does not manage what is not hers.

Even when she knows exactly how.

And in that restraint, she remains fully herself.

Chapter 26

Desire Is Not Negotiable

There was a time when she believed desire could be maintained.

Not felt, not waited for, but managed.

If things slowed down, she adjusted. If distance appeared, she responded. If something felt off, she bridged it.

She did not think of this as negotiation. She thought of it as effort. As care.

As part of keeping a relationship alive.

But over time, something became clear.

Desire does not respond to effort in that way.

The Quiet Substitution

What replaced desire was not always obvious.

There was still intimacy. Still closeness. Still the appearance of connection.

But the source had changed.

It was no longer arising from wanting.

It was arising from intention.

From maintenance.

From the subtle understanding that this was something that needed to continue.

And so it did.

Not because she wanted to. But because she knew how.

The Difference Between Willing and Wanting

This is where the distinction begins.

She was willing.

Often.

Willing to meet him where he was. Willing to participate. Willing to maintain what seemed important to the relationship.

But willingness is not the same as desire.

Willingness can be generated. It can be accessed through thought, through care, through a sense of responsibility.

Desire cannot.

Desire either exists, or it does not.

No More Maintenance Intimacy

This is what she no longer does.

She does not use intimacy to stabilize the relationship.

She does not offer her body to smooth over tension, to prevent distance, to restore closeness that has been disrupted elsewhere.

She does not move toward him out of fear that not doing so will create a gap.

Because she understands now: what is created that way does not last.

And what it costs her accumulates.

No More Keeping the Peace

There was a time when she believed this was generosity.

To say yes when she could have said no.

To move toward connection when she felt neutral.

To prioritize the relationship over the exact truth of her own desire.

It felt like maturity. Like being someone who understood how relationships worked.

But what it created was something else.

A quiet dissonance. A gap between what she was doing—and what she was feeling.

And over time, that gap widened.

The Body Knows

Even when the mind explains, the body registers.

It knows when something is chosen.

And when something is complied with.

It knows the difference between wanting and participating. Between presence and performance.

And it stores that difference.

Not as a single moment. But as a pattern.

The Return to Autonomy

This is where something changes.

She begins to experience her body differently.

Not as something that must be responsive.

Not as something that must be available.

But as something that belongs to her. Fully.

Not in theory. In practice.

Erotic Autonomy

This is not withdrawal.

It is not rejection of intimacy.

It is ownership.

The understanding that desire is not something she owes.

Not something she provides in exchange for stability, connection, or approval.

It is something she either feels, or does not.

And both are allowed.

The End of Negotiation

She no longer negotiates with herself.

She does not persuade herself into wanting.

She does not reason her way into readiness.

She does not override hesitation in order to maintain something.

If the desire is not there—she does not replace it with effort.

The Space This Creates

At first, this can feel uncertain.

There are pauses where there was once movement. Moments where something would have happened, but does not.

The rhythm changes.

But in that space, something else becomes possible.

Honesty.

Desire, Unforced
When desire does appear, it feels different.

Not managed. Not anticipated.

Unforced.

It arises without strategy.

Without purpose beyond itself.

And because it is not being used to do anything—it feels alive again.

Choosing Slowness
She no longer moves ahead of herself.

She allows time. She allows uncertainty. She allows desire to arrive, or not, without immediately responding to its absence.

There is no urgency.

No need to prove that something is still there.

What is there will show itself.

The End of Performance

She is no longer performing enthusiasm.

No longer mirroring what she believes is expected.

No longer shaping her responses to maintain a particular version of the relationship.

If she wants—she moves toward.

If she does not—she does not.

Mutuality

This is where the standard becomes clear.

Desire must be mutual.

Not negotiated. Not compensated for. Not balanced through effort on one side.

Mutual.

Or absent.

And if it is absent—that absence matters.

It is not something to be worked around indefinitely.

The Courage in This

This requires something she did not have before.

The willingness to let the moment remain unresolved.

The willingness to let the relationship reveal its reality.

The willingness to not intervene.

Because she understands now: forcing what is not there does not preserve connection.

It distorts it.

The Reclaiming

This is not only about intimacy.

It is about self-trust.

The ability to feel something, and not override it. To notice hesitation, and not immediately correct it. To recognize absence, and not replace it with effort.

She trusts her experience. Even when it is inconvenient. Even when it creates tension.

What This Chapter Is Saying

Desire cannot be sustained through obligation.

It cannot be maintained through effort alone.

It cannot survive where it is being asked to serve a function beyond itself.

The Final Truth

Desire is not negotiated.

It is either present, or it is not.

When it is real, it does not need to be managed.

It moves on its own.

And so does she.

Chapter 27

Paying Attention to the Shift

It does not begin with something obvious.

There is no clear event, no moment that justifies concern. Nothing she could point to and say, this is where it changed.

What she notices instead is smaller, quieter—far easier to dismiss. A tone that lands slightly differently. A pause that lingers a little longer than it used to. A response that feels just off enough to register, but not enough to confront.

Before, she would have let it pass.

The Micro-Change
This is where it always begins.

Not with collapse, but with a shift—subtle, almost imperceptible, easy to explain away.

He is tired. He's stressed. It's been a long week.

These explanations are not necessarily wrong. But they are not the point.

The point is that something changed.

Before, she would have prioritized continuity over curiosity, smoothing the moment, adjusting her response, restoring the previous rhythm before it could break.

She believed this was stability. But what it actually did was delay visibility.

The pattern did not disappear. It formed slowly, without interruption, built from moments that were felt but not acknowledged.

Not Waiting for the Pattern

What she does differently now is simple, but not easy.

She does not wait for the pattern to fully form. She does not wait until it is undeniable—until it has repeated enough times to justify concern, until it can be explained clearly to someone else.

She pays attention earlier, at the first shift.

She feels it not as a conclusion, but as a sensation. Something slightly misaligned, something not quite landing.

It would be easy to dismiss, and for a long time, she did. But now she treats that feeling differently.

Discomfort as Data

Her discomfort is not something to correct or minimize.

It is information.

It is telling her something about what is happening, about what is changing, about what may be forming beneath the surface.

Instead of overriding it, she stays with it.

She does not rush to act. She does not confront or escalate.

But she does not ignore it either. She allows the moment to remain unresolved, not as something to fix, but as something to observe.

Interrupting the Slow Slide

This is what prevents the pattern from taking hold.

Patterns require time. They require repetition, and they rely on moments being absorbed without being examined.

By paying attention early, she disrupts that process. She does not allow something to build unnoticed.

She also no longer rushes to create a narrative that makes the moment easier to accept. She does not soften what she feels in order to preserve the relationship. If something feels off, she lets it be off, without immediately restoring it to neutral.

Trusting the First Signal

This is not about becoming suspicious.

It is about becoming attentive.

It is not about assuming the worst, but about not overriding the first signal. Because she understands now that the first signal is often the most honest, before it is explained away, before it is rationalized, before it is absorbed into something familiar.

In doing this, she creates space for clarity. Not instantly, but over time. Because she is no longer interfering with what is unfolding, she is able to see it more accurately.

The Final Truth

You do not need to wait for something to become obvious before you take it seriously.

You do not need a pattern to justify your attention.

The first shift is enough.

She pays attention when something changes—not after, not once it has settled into something she can no longer ignore, but at the beginning.

And because of that, she no longer finds herself years into something she recognized—quietly—from the start.

Chapter 28

The Liberation of Doing Less, and Watching What Happens

There was a time when she believed effort was what made a relationship work.

If something felt off, she leaned in. If there was distance, she closed it. If something was missing, she supplied it. Not dramatically, not in ways that could be easily named, but consistently.

She adjusted, anticipated, compensated.

And because she did, the relationship held together.

The Instinct to Step In

The instinct is still there.

She still sees what is missing. She still notices the gap before it widens, the moment before it turns into something more difficult. She knows exactly what she could do to restore ease, bring things back into balance, make the interaction smoother.

For a long time, she acted on that instinct immediately.

She believed that was what care looked like.

What She Does Differently

Now, she pauses. Not because she is unsure, but because she is no longer willing to compensate for what is not being offered.

She does less. She does not fill the silence as quickly, initiate every repair, or supply what has not been given.

The instinct rises, as it always did.

And she lets it pass.

Stepping Back Instead of Stepping In

This is the shift.

Before, she moved toward the gap. Now, she steps back from it.

She allows the moment to exist without immediately changing it. She allows things to be slightly uneven, slightly unresolved, slightly unclear.

Not as a strategy. But as a refusal to carry what is not hers.

Allowing the Gap to Appear

When she stops compensating, something becomes visible.

The gap she once filled does not disappear.

It remains.

What she once smoothed over now sits in the open, without being immediately corrected.

This can feel uncomfortable at first. There is a pull to restore the previous rhythm, to make it feel normal again, to remove the tension.

But she does not move to close it. She lets it show itself.

The Discomfort of Non-Intervention

This is where it becomes real.

Because doing less does not feel like ease at first.

It feels like restraint.

She feels the moment stretch—the absence of her usual response, the lack of immediate repair. She notices the space where she would have stepped in, and she feels the urge to do so.

And she stays still. Not out of indifference, but out of clarity.

What Over-Functioning Hid

Before, her effort made things look more balanced than they were.

Her anticipation covered the absence of his. Her responsiveness compensated for what was not being initiated. Her consistency stabilized what might otherwise have faltered.

She was not only participating in the relationship. She was holding it together.

And because she was doing that, it was difficult to see what would happen if she stopped.

What Reveals Itself

Now, she does stop.

And without her constant input, the dynamic becomes clearer.

What is there remains.

What is not there does not appear.

There is no longer a layer of effort disguising the structure underneath.

This is not about testing him. It is about no longer testing herself.

The End of Quiet Compensation

She no longer fills in what is missing in order to preserve the feeling of connection.

If something is not initiated, it remains uninitiated. If something is not addressed, it remains visible.

She does not rush to restore equilibrium.

Because she understands now: the equilibrium she created was not always real.

Letting the Relationship Stand

For the first time, she allows the relationship to stand on its own.

Not supported by her extra effort. Not stabilized by her anticipation. Not held together by her willingness to do more.

What remains is what is actually there.

The Internal Shift

This is not about withdrawing.

She is still present, still engaged, still responsive when something is genuinely mutual.

But she is no longer extending herself beyond that. She is no longer moving ahead of the relationship to ensure it continues to function.

She meets what is given. And nothing more.

The Clarity That Follows

When she does less, she sees more.

Not because anything new has appeared, but because nothing is being concealed.

The absence is no longer covered. The imbalance is no longer softened. The dynamic is no longer adjusted into something easier to live with.

It is simply visible.

What This Chapter Is Saying

Doing more does not always create more.

Sometimes, it hides what is missing.

And when she stops over-functioning, she is not breaking the relationship.

She is allowing it to show itself.

The Final Truth
She does less.

Not to withdraw. Not to punish. Not to create distance.

But to stop carrying what was never hers to begin with.

In that space, she sees what she is actually standing in.

And in seeing it—she is free.

Chapter 29

Not Staying to See If It Gets Better

Why Waiting is Denial Dressed as Patience

There was a time when she believed in waiting.

Not passively, not without awareness, but with a quiet conviction that time would clarify things. That if she stayed present, patient, open, something would shift. That what felt slightly off would settle, that what was missing would emerge, that what was inconsistent would stabilize.

Waiting felt reasonable. It felt mature. It felt like what you do when you care about something enough not to walk away too quickly.

The "Wait and See" Logic
The reasoning is familiar:
It's early.
It's just a phase.
Things will even out.
Nothing is clearly wrong.
Nothing is severe enough to justify leaving.
There is still potential.

And so she stays.

Not because she is unaware.

But because she is hopeful.

The Subtle Cost of Waiting

Waiting is often *denial dressed as patience.*

What waiting does over time is shift her position.

Instead of responding to what is actually happening, she begins to orient herself toward what *might* happen.

Instead of evaluating the relationship as it is, she begins to evaluate it as it could be.

And in that shift, something important is lost.

Clarity.

The Pull of Potential

Potential is persuasive.

It offers a version of the relationship that feels just within reach. A future that seems possible if the right adjustments are made, if the right conversations happen, if enough time is given.

She does not imagine something unrealistic. She extrapolates from what she has already seen.

The moments of connection. The glimpses of what could work.

And she builds around that.

Loyalty to What Is Not Yet Real

This is where she stays longer than she should. Not because of what is consistently present. But because of what appears intermittently.

She becomes loyal to a version of the relationship that is not fully realized.

A version that requires time, effort, and alignment to become stable.

And she tells herself that it is worth waiting for.

What She Understands Now

Patterns do not need time to form. They reveal themselves early.

Not in their full expression. But in their direction.

The way someone shows up. The way they respond. The way they participate, or do not.

These things do not transform completely with time.

They become more established.

Patterns Do Not Self-Correct

This is what she sees clearly now.

What is present at the beginning is not incidental. It is foundational.

It may soften. It may fluctuate.

But it does not fundamentally reorganize itself without deliberate, sustained change.

And waiting, on its own, does not create that change.

The Cost of Staying to Find Out

Every time she stays to see if it will get better, she invests more. More time. More energy. More emotional commitment.

And as that investment grows, it becomes harder to leave.

Not because the relationship has improved. But because she has become more attached to the outcome.

The Shift From Hope to Clarity

What she does differently now is subtle.

She still notices potential. But she does not prioritize it over reality.

She pays attention to what is consistent. What is actually happening. What is already present without being prompted or sustained by her effort.

And she evaluates based on that.

No More Waiting for Alignment

If something feels misaligned, she does not immediately assume it will resolve.

She allows the misalignment to be seen. She gives it space to either shift or remain.

But she does not anchor herself to the expectation that it will improve simply because she stays.

The End of Earned Outcomes

Before, there was an implicit belief. That if she showed up well enough, communicated clearly enough, remained patient enough—the relationship would evolve in response.

That her presence could influence the trajectory.

Now, she understands something different.

Her effort can reveal the relationship. But it cannot transform it into something it is not.

Choosing What Is, Not What Could Be

This is the core shift.

She chooses based on what is consistently available. Not on what might become available with time.

She does not build a future on intermittent evidence. She responds to what is already established.

What This Chapter Is Saying

Waiting is not neutral.

It shapes how long you stay inside something that is not fully working.

It delays decisions that are already forming.

And it often binds you more tightly to something that has not fundamentally changed.

The Final Truth

She does not stay to see if it gets better.

She sees what is already there.

And she decides—without waiting for it to become something else.

Chapter 30

Being Willing to Lose the Relationship

There was a time when the possibility of losing the relationship shaped everything.

Not always consciously, not in a way she would have named directly, but quietly, persistently—in the background of her decisions.

It influenced what she said and what she withheld, what she addressed and what she let pass, how much she adjusted, how quickly she moved to restore connection when something felt uncertain.

She did not think of herself as afraid. She thought of herself as committed.

The Subtle Fear Beneath It

The fear was not dramatic.

It did not present as panic or desperation. It appeared in smaller, more socially acceptable forms. A desire to keep things good. A preference for harmony. A willingness to meet in the middle, even when the middle kept shifting.

But underneath those behaviors was something steady.

If this breaks, I lose something important.

And so, in spite of her resentment, she oriented herself toward preservation.

How Fear Shapes Behavior
Fear does not always look like clinging.

Often, it looks like competence.

She becomes easier to be with. More accommodating. More understanding.

She anticipates what might create distance and moves to prevent it. She notices early signs of disconnection and responds quickly. She smooths, softens, stabilizes.

Not because she is weak—but because she is trying to keep something from being lost.

The Performance of Security
Over time, this creates a version of her that appears secure.

She is calm. Reasonable. Adaptable.

But beneath that is constant adjustment.

A quiet effort to maintain the relationship in a particular state.

She is not being herself freely. She is being herself carefully. And the resentment builds.

The Turning Point

This is what changes.

Not the relationship first.

Her relationship to losing it.

She becomes willing. Not eager. Not indifferent.

But willing.

Willing for the relationship to end if it requires her to override herself in order to continue it.

The End of Fear-Based Attachment

This is the shift everything else depends on.

As long as she is afraid of losing him, she will adapt.

She will soften what she feels, adjust what she wants, minimize what is missing. She will prioritize keeping the relationship over being fully present within it.

When that fear lifts, even slightly, something else becomes possible.

Honesty.

What Changes in Real Time

She speaks without rehearsing how it will land.

She allows disagreement without immediately resolving it.

She lets moments remain incomplete, without rushing to restore connection.

She does not move to secure the relationship at every point of tension.

And this changes the dynamic immediately.

No Performance to Avoid Abandonment

Before, there was an implicit contract: if I show up well enough, this will hold.

Now, that contract is gone.

She does not perform stability, manufacture ease, or adjust herself in advance to prevent loss.

She allows the relationship to respond to who she actually is.

The Risk in This

This is not without consequence.

The relationship may not hold.

When she stops compensating, stops performing, stops organizing herself around preservation, what remains is no longer supported in the same way.

And that can reveal a truth she was previously buffering.

Why This Is the Turning Point

Because everything before this still contains negotiation. Even awareness. Even restraint.

But as long as the underlying fear remains, there is still a subtle pull to adapt.

This is the point where that pull weakens.

She is no longer choosing her behavior based on what will keep the relationship intact.

She is choosing based on what is true.

The Internal Stability

What replaces fear is not certainty about the relationship.

It is stability within herself.

The understanding that she will be intact even if the relationship ends.

That losing him is not the same as losing herself.

And because of that, she no longer needs to prevent every possible point of rupture.

What This Chapter Is Saying

A relationship that can only exist if you adjust yourself continuously is not stable.

It is maintained.

And maintenance driven by fear will always require more of you over time.

The Final Truth

She is willing to lose the resentment. She is willing to lose the relationship.

Not because it does not matter.

But because *she* does.

And she is no longer willing to disappear to keep something that cannot hold her as she is.

Chapter 31

Recognizing the Pattern, Not the Person

Different Partner, Same Pattern

For a long time, she believed the problem was *who* she chose.

That if she could just choose better, everything would be different.

A different man, a different personality, a different dynamic. Someone more emotionally available, more communicative, more aligned.

And sometimes, she did choose differently. The details changed. The personality changed.

The surface of the relationship looked new.

But something familiar returned. Not immediately. Not in the beginning.

But eventually.

The Familiar Feeling

It did not always look the same. The circumstances were different. The behaviors were different. The language was different.

But the feeling was familiar.

The sense of doing more. The sense of adjusting. The quiet awareness that she was once again carrying something that was not being equally held.

And that is when something begins to shift.

The Pattern Beneath the Person

She starts to see what she did not see before.

That the common denominator is not the man.

It is the *dynamic*.

The structure of how the relationship forms, how it stabilizes, how it continues.

And within that structure—*her role*.

Different Man, Same Pattern

This is the recognition that changes everything.

That it can look different on the surface and still function the same underneath.

That she can be with someone new and still find herself in the same position.

More aware, perhaps. More articulate.

But still compensating. Still adjusting. Still maintaining.

Why It Repeats

Patterns are not created at the point of conflict.

They are created at the beginning.

In what is tolerated. In what is overlooked. In what is adjusted early in order to create ease.

Patterns form quietly. Before anything is wrong enough to question.

And once they are established, they are difficult to undo without disrupting the entire structure.

Seeing It Earlier

This is what she does differently now.

She does not focus only on who he is.

She pays attention to how the dynamic is forming. Who is initiating. Who is adjusting. Who is noticing. Who is carrying.

She watches the movement between them. Not just the individual in front of her.

The Shift in Attention

Before, she evaluated based on qualities. Is he kind? Is he attentive? Is he interested?

Now, she evaluates based on patterns. What happens when something is unclear? What happens when there is a gap? What happens when she does not step in?

She watches for structure.

Early Signals of the Old Pattern

The signs are not dramatic. They rarely are.

They appear in small moments. Moments in which she could intervene and smooth something—and notices that she wants to. Moments where she feels the pull to adjust, to make something easier, to keep the connection steady.

She recognizes the feeling. Not as chemistry. But as familiarity.

The Difference Between Attraction and Recognition

This is an important distinction.

Not everything that feels familiar is aligned.

Sometimes, familiarity is the pattern repeating.

The pull toward dynamics she already knows how to navigate. Where she knows how to function. Where she knows how to be effective.

But effectiveness is not the same as mutuality.

Recognition Over Repetition

There is a reason the first moment often carries more clarity than everything that follows. Before it is explained away. Before it is softened by context, by empathy, by the desire to make something work.

The first signal is usually clean.

What comes after is interpretation.

She has learned this now. That she does not need repetition to confirm what she already felt. That seeing it once is often enough.

Not because people cannot change.

But because patterns rarely hide. They introduce themselves early, and then wait to see if they will be ignored.

Interrupting the Pattern

Now, when she notices that pull, she does not follow it automatically.

She slows down. She does less. She allows the interaction to unfold without stepping into her usual role.

And she watches.

The End of Personalizing Everything

She no longer assumes that what is happening is about him alone. Or about her alone.

She sees the interaction.

The space between them.

And how it is being shaped.

What This Changes

This removes something she carried for a long time.

The belief that if she could just find the right person, the pattern would disappear.

Now, she understands that the pattern requires her participation.

And that means it can also be interrupted by her.

What This Chapter Is Saying

The goal is not to find a completely different person.

It is to *not recreate the same dynamic.*

Because without that awareness, the pattern will repeat—even in a relationship that looks entirely different.

The Final Truth

She recognizes the pattern, not just the person.

And because of that, she no longer mistakes familiarity for alignment.

Chapter 32

SELF-TRUST AFTER RESENTMENT

There is a moment, after everything has settled, when the question changes.

It is no longer about him.

Not about what he did, or did not do. Not about what the relationship was, or could have been. Not even about whether it ended in the right way.

The question becomes quieter: *Can I trust myself now?*

After the Clarity

Resentment brings clarity, but it comes late.

By the time she sees the pattern fully, she has already lived inside it. She has already adapted, already explained things away, already stayed past the point where something in her knew.

And that creates a different kind of discomfort. Not just about what happened—but about what she allowed.

The Temptation to Soften the Past

This is where the mind tries to restore comfort.

It revisits the relationship and rearranges it slightly. It emphasizes the good, reframes the difficult, smooths the edges of what felt sharp at the time.

It says: it wasn't that bad. There were good moments. Maybe I expected too much.

And some of this may be true.

But it is not the full truth.

Why We Rewrite

Rewriting the past makes it easier to live with.

If the relationship was not as imbalanced as it felt, then staying longer makes sense. If the pattern was not as clear, then missing it feels less significant.

It protects her from something more difficult.

The recognition that she saw more than she admitted.

Holding the Full Picture

Self-trust requires something different.

The ability to hold the whole experience without editing it.

To remember the good without using it to erase the difficult. To acknowledge the connection without denying the cost.

To see the pattern clearly—even when it is uncomfortable to admit how long it was tolerated.

Not Punishing, Not Excusing

This is not about blaming herself.

But it is also not about absolving herself through distortion.

She does not need to punish who she was then.

But she also does not need to protect that version of herself from the truth.

She can understand why she stayed.

And still recognize that something in her knew.

The Pull of Nostalgia

This is where the risk returns.

Not in the form of the relationship as it was. But as it is remembered.

Time softens things. Distance removes friction.

What remains are the moments that felt good, the parts that worked, the version of the relationship that was easiest to hold.

And this creates a quiet pull.

Not always to go back physically. But to return psychologically. To reconsider. To reinterpret. To reopen something that felt unfinished.

Nostalgia Is Selective

It does not replay the full experience.

It does not include the exhaustion. The quiet resentment. The feeling of carrying something alone.

It presents a version that is easier to miss.

And if she is not careful, she can mistake that version for reality.

Not Returning to the Pattern

This is where self-trust becomes active.

She notices the pull. She recognizes the softness in how she is remembering.

And she stays with what she knows.

Not the most comforting version.

The most accurate one.

She does not return to something that required her to override herself.

Not because it was all bad. But because it was not fully right.

Trusting What She Knew Then

This is the most important shift.

She begins to trust the version of herself who felt the discomfort in real time.

The one who noticed the imbalance. The one who felt the misalignment before it became undeniable.

The one who knew—even when she did not act on it immediately.

That version of her is not unreliable.

It is the most honest one.

The Repair

Self-trust is not rebuilt through certainty.

It is rebuilt through recognition.

Through seeing clearly what happened, without distortion. Through acknowledging where she overrode herself. Through choosing differently now.

Not perfectly. But consciously.

What This Chapter Is Saying

You do not rebuild trust in yourself by pretending you did not see what you saw.

You rebuild it by honoring it.

Even if you did not act on it at the time.

The Final Truth

She does not rewrite the past to make it easier to carry. She remembers it accurately.

And because of that, she no longer returns to what once required her to leave herself behind.

Chapter 33

No Longer Living in Disappearance

There was a time when she believed this was simply how life worked.

Adjustment. Flexibility. The ability to move around other people's needs, to anticipate what was required before it was asked, to make things work—even when they did not quite fit.

It did not feel like disappearance. It felt like competence.

She was capable. Reliable. Someone who held things together.

And because of that, she was valued.

The Shape of a Life

Over time, this did not remain contained to one relationship.

It extended beyond it.

Into her work, where she took on more than was asked, noticed what others missed, and filled gaps without needing recognition.

Into her friendships, where she was the one who remembered, reached out, and held emotional continuity.

Into her identity, where being the one who could manage, adapt, and sustain became part of how she understood herself.

She built a life that functioned.

But within it, something was consistently being asked of her: Less of herself.

The Subtle Disappearance

It did not happen all at once.

It happened in increments.

A preference set aside here. A boundary softened there. A moment of discomfort overridden in order to maintain ease.

Each individual moment was small.

But over time, they accumulated into something structural.

A life that required her to adjust in order to remain inside it.

What She Sees Now

This is what becomes clear.

That the issue was never just the relationship. It was the pattern she brought into everything.

The instinct to accommodate before being asked.

To stabilize before something had fully revealed itself.

To take responsibility for what was not hers in order to keep things functioning.

And because she was capable of doing this, she did it everywhere.

The Cost of Being the One Who Can
Competence is rarely questioned.

When she could do more, she was often expected to.

When she could carry more, it became easy for others to let her.

Not always consciously. Not always intentionally. But consistently.

And because she did not always name the cost, it continued.

The Turning Point
This is where something shifted.

Not in one dramatic decision. But in a series of refusals.

She began to notice where her life required her to override herself in order to maintain it.

And she stopped agreeing to that requirement.

In Relationships
She does not stay where she must constantly adjust to remain.

She does not build connection through over-functioning.

She allows the relationship to meet her as she is—or not hold.

In Work
She notices where she is carrying more than is hers.

She sees where her competence has turned into expectation.

And she begins to step back.

Not by withdrawing entirely. But by no longer filling every gap automatically.

She allows responsibility to distribute itself.

In Identity
This is where the shift is most subtle.

She begins to loosen her attachment to being the one who can always manage. Always adapt. Always make things work.

Because she understands now that this identity was built, in part, on self-abandonment.

The Reorientation
She asks a different question.

Not: Can I make this work?

But: Can I be fully myself here?

And if the answer is no—she does not immediately try to change herself to make the answer yes.

The End of Self-Abandonment

This does not mean she never compromises.

It means she no longer disappears.

There is a difference.

Compromise adjusts. Disappearance erases.

She knows that difference now.

What She Builds Instead

She begins, slowly, to build a life that does not depend on her absence.

Where her preferences are included.

Where her boundaries are not continually negotiated down.

Where her presence does not require constant adjustment.

This is not perfect. But it is aligned.

The Integration

Everything she has learned comes together here.

The awareness of patterns. The refusal to over-function. The willingness to lose what does not hold. The trust in her own experience.

It is no longer something she applies selectively.

It becomes how she lives.

What This Chapter Is Saying

A relationship is not the only place where self-abandonment occurs.

It is a pattern that can shape an entire life.

And when that pattern is no longer maintained—everything begins to reorganize.

The Final Truth

She does not build a life that requires her to disappear.

Not in love. Not in work. Not in who she is.

And because of that, she no longer has to fight to remain visible inside it.

Desire does not become duty here.

Because she no longer builds a life that requires it.

Resentment does not arrive all at once.

It builds quietly, over time, in moments that do not seem significant on their own.

A small accommodation. A softened boundary. A yes that should have been a no. A silence where something should have been said.

Individually, these moments are easy to dismiss.

Together, they form something structural.

By the time resentment is fully felt, it is rarely about one thing.

It is about *accumulation.*

About the distance between what was felt and what was expressed. Between what was needed and what was given. Between who she was—and who she became in order to sustain the relationship.

This book has been an examination of that distance.

Not to assign blame, and not to simplify something inherently complex, but to name what is often experienced and rarely articulated clearly.

The resentment years are not a failure of love.

They are the result of a pattern.

A pattern of over-functioning. Of anticipating. Of adjusting. Of taking responsibility for what was not hers to carry.

A pattern often rewarded early, often mistaken for strength, and often sustained long after it begins to cost something essential.

What changes is not the existence of that pattern.

It is the recognition of it.

Because once it is seen, it cannot be unseen.

She begins to notice it in real time. In the moment she moves to adjust before she has been asked. In the instinct to stabilize something that has not been offered equally. In the quiet urge to maintain connection at the expense of her own clarity.

And gradually, she does something different.

Not perfectly. Not all at once.

But consistently enough that the pattern no longer runs uninterrupted.

She pauses.

She pays attention. She does less. She allows the relationship—and her life—to reveal themselves without her constant intervention.

And in that space, something becomes clear.

What is mutual remains.

What is not, does not hold in the same way.

This is not always comfortable.

It may lead to change. It may lead to loss.

But it also leads to something else.

Alignment.

The kind that does not require constant maintenance. The kind that does not depend on her adjusting herself in order to sustain it.

The kind that allows her to remain present, rather than perform presence.

The resentment does not disappear all at once.

There is no single moment where everything resolves. No clean point where the pattern disappears entirely.

It changes the same way it was built. Gradually. Quietly. Through small decisions that no longer go unnoticed.

And over time, it no longer accumulates in the same way.

Because the conditions that created it are no longer being repeated.

This is the shift.

Not in finding a perfect relationship. Not in avoiding difficulty. But in no longer living in a way that requires her to override herself in order to remain inside it.

That is what resolves the resentment years.

Not by erasing them. But by understanding them—and choosing differently from that understanding.

She did not become harder to love.

She became unwilling to perform for it.

And because of that—the resentment years end here.

This is not a "how to be happy ever after" book.

You didn't become resentful overnight. And you do not return to yourself overnight either.

But now—you know exactly where you left.

And you no longer leave yourself there again.

About the Author

Mina V. Adler

Mina V. Adler writes about sex, power, and the slow burn of resentment no one warns you about.

With sharp psychological insight and uncompromising honesty, Adler exposes the invisible expectations that shape modern relationships—especially the subtle pressure many women feel to maintain sexual availability in order to keep the peace, preserve connection, or prevent distance.

With zero tolerance for self-abandonment, she pulls apart the fantasy of modern relationships and shows what's really going on underneath.

Her message is simple: you don't keep love by performing for it—and you don't owe your body to hold it together.

By the Same Author

Die Alone, Then

The Loneliness Lie & Why Peace Outweighs Partnership

There is a "threat" society keeps using against women. "Lower your standards or you'll die alone!"

Women are conditioned to believe that those of us who expect too much from men or relationships – even when it isn't much at all – will end up alone.

Promises, promises. As if being alone in peace is worse than being miserable with someone.

Being alone doesn't mean being lonely. I've never felt more lonely and quietly desperate than when I was partnered with a man who disrespected and drained me.

The Pros of being alone far outweigh the Cons. The tidy home. The clean bathroom. The calm nervous systems and mental clarity. The balanced PH. The supportive friends. The conviction that You Are Enough. A peace and serenity like no other. That, to me sounds like liberation.

Society audaciously tells women to settle. To accept less. To tolerate disrespect, weaponized incompetence, emotional unavailability, and lack of effort. Just to avoid being single. That, to me, sounds more like punishment.

Men love throwing "you'll die alone" at women who have standards, but what they're really saying is: "Lower your expectations so I don't have to improve." They want access to high-value women without being high-value men. They want partnership benefits without partnership effort.

And when women refuse? They shame us with loneliness threats as if we're not watching married women be lonelier than single ones.

So yes, if having standards means being "alone" with peace, health, cleanliness, and supportive friends, women will choose that every time.

Being alone isn't the threat men think it is anymore. Being with the wrong person? That's the real nightmare.

Women better relax? No. Without unworthy men, women are finally relaxed.

This unapologetic non-fiction guide for women reveals the hidden worlds, habits, histories, and emotional architectures many men keep tucked away. It aims to empower women, rather than breed suspicion or resentment.

The Secret Lives of Men will give you the tools to see clearly, demand honesty, set boundaries, and reclaim your emotional power.

No compromises. No excuses. No apologies.

This is not a war on men, nor a work on the psychology of men. It's about the impact of men's secrets on women. It's a wake-up call for women tired of making excuses, feeling hurt, absorbing the fallout, and rationalizing patterns that undermine their lives.

It's time to stop paying the price for male secrecy—and start living on your terms.